WINNING JEWS
TO CHRIST

WINNING JEWS TO CHRIST

A HANDBOOK TO AID CHRISTIANS IN THEIR APPROACH TO THE JEWS

by
JACOB GARTENHAUS, D.D., LITT.D.

SWORD OF THE LORD PUBLISHERS
MURFREESBORO, TENNESSEE 37130

This book has previously been published in the following editions:

First Edition—*Winning Jews to Christ* (1963),
Zondervan Publishing House

Second Edition—*Unto His Own* (1965),
Marshall, Morgan and Scott

Third Edition—*Unto His Own* (1967),
Christian Literature Crusade

This Edition—*Winning Jews to Christ* (1976),
Sword of the Lord Publishers

This book is also available in Spanish and Portuguese.

ISBN 0-87398-925-2

Printed in the United States of America

I gratefully dedicate this edition to my many friends and faithful supporters whose sacrificial giving through the years has made it possible for this ministry of carrying the Gospel of Christ "to the Jew first, and also to the Greek" to expand into a world-wide ministry.

Jacob Gartenhaus

FOREWORD

Without hesitancy I say that *Winning Jews to Christ* by Dr. Jacob Gartenhaus is a storehouse of information concerning the Jewish people, their history as a peculiar people, the Jewish religion and their prayer life, the Jewish feasts and Jewish fasts, the Jewish laws and customs, the Jewish literature—and many other pertinent truths about this unique people. These truths which so few know and which all peoples should learn are set forth with a meticulous accuracy that gets and holds the attention of the reader—whether the reader be friend or foe of the Jews, whether he be one of average education or a scholar.

Reading this book one is made to think of a diver who goes repeatedly down into pearl beds and comes up with pearls filling both hands.

With attractive, yea, with entrancing language, Dr. Gartenhaus has made known to us truths about the Jewish people of which many have been ignorant. This book will bring informative blessing, refreshing inspiration, and an acknowledgment of our indebtedness to the Jewish people through whom came our Messiah and the Bible. The readers will find in it a gold mine of helpful suggestions on how to present to the Jew the "Good News" tactfully and efficiently, and how to refute his various objections, doctrinal and historical. This book ought to be in the library of all preachers in all pulpits and synagogues, of all teachers in all seminaries, and all colleges. To fail or to refuse to read it is to rob one of that which enriches. I predict for this book a wide sale, a wide reading, and great usefulness.

Robert G. Lee

Memphis, Tennessee

INTRODUCTION

In my opinion, this volume for which I have the privilege of writing an introductory word is unique in the field of Jewish evangelism, actually, in the literature of the whole field of evangelism. Beginning with the great upsurge of missionary activity among Jewish people both in Western Europe and in Great Britain, especially in London, at the middle of the nineteenth century, a very important literature has been produced, more extensive than at any other period of church history. Some of these titles have for their main purpose the urging of evangelical Christians to undertake seriously the difficult task of evangelizing the Jews. Other volumes have been written either attempting to write the history of Jewish evangelization, or the history of certain societies engaged in this work, as the British Society for the Propagation of the Gospel Among the Jews, the oldest Jewish Mission Society in the world, with which organization Dr. Gartenhaus is closely affiliated. The purpose of others is to present biographical sketches of some of the outstanding Hebrew Christians of modern times, a very important and interesting subject. Personally, however, I do not know of any volume in the English language which in a really thoroughgoing manner attempts to give to Christians burdened for the cause of Jewish evangelization a knowledge of the customs, the outlook, the literature, convictions and hopes of the modern Jew as our author has, in a masterly way, done in this volume.

Moreover, he acquaints us with the Jewish conceptions and attitudes toward non-Jews, especially toward Christianity and its author, Jesus. He further gives us most valuable suggestions as to how to approach the various types of Jews, how to gain entrance into their highly sensitive, suspicious and apprehensive hearts and minds, how to gain their confidence and arouse their interest in the claims of Christ to be the Messiah.

Dr. Jacob Gartenhaus has the five basic qualities necessary for the writing of any work like this with firsthand knowledge and as it were with authority. First of all, he was born and continues to be, of course, a Jew, who by upbringing, education, and association has an intimate acquaintance with the ancient as well as the modern customs of Jews, knows the literature, can read the language, and can enter sympathetically into the opinions, practices, hopes and longings of this ancient people. He knows what a Jew will find appealing in the Christian Gospel, and he also knows what to avoid that would antagonize him.

In the second place, our author is a devout Christian. He has a living experience with the Messiah of Israel, who is the fulfillment of the prophecies, the author of eternal salvation, son of David and son of God, the only Saviour of men. In the third place, and this is not true I think of all the redeemed, not even of all the redeemed of Israel, our author has a great love for his people, and a Pauline longing to see many of this chosen but bewildered race saved through Christ.

In addition to these factors of such great importance, he, as is clearly revealed in these pages, has a gift for research, for the organization of material, a gift for teaching with clearness the subjects he here undertakes to discuss which are in many cases difficult and often so misunderstood. Finally, Doctor Gartenhaus has in this volume as it were given us the mature results of years of unceasing devotion to the very type of work to which he hopes a great multitude of earnest believers will be drawn. This is not the product of the dreams of a commendably eager but young and untried evangelist among the Jews, but of one who by the grace of God has been abundantly used through the years in leading many of his own people to receive Jesus as their Messiah, and to come into an experience of full salvation through Christ.

Dr. Gartenhaus is a graduate of the Moody Bible Institute, Chicago, Illinois, and the Southern Baptist Theological Seminary, Louisville, Kentucky. His rich experience in his world-wide ministry, his indefatigable and selfless activities in the Master's vineyard, have earned for him the love and esteem of all who have come to know him. In recognition of his unique contribution and achievements, Georgetown College, Georgetown, Kentucky, conferred upon Dr. Gartenhaus the degree of Doctor of Divinity, and Union University, Jackson, Tennessee, the degree of Doctor of Literature. And I am sure that the greatest of all degrees is yet in store for him, that is, the words of our Saviour, "Well done, thou good and faithful servant," which the Master bestows on those who do His work well.

I may add here that Dr. Gartenhaus is a prolific writer of books, tracts and articles which have had a wide circulation and many editions. His style is clear, concise and to the point so that it may be understood by all.

I hope and pray that this book will arouse the hearts of many Christians to seriously consider the tremendous importance of lovingly and intelligently presenting the Gospel to these children of Abraham, the brethren of our Lord.

—WILBUR M. SMITH

CONTENTS

Foreword by *Dr. Robert G. Lee*

Introduction by *Dr. Wilbur M. Smith*

" Cappee 'ai" yarmulka' shull cap (handwritten note)

CHAPTER I

THE STIRRING OF THE BONES

Why such a manual?

Why should we care about Judaism? Why study Judaism? Are there not already enough books on this subject?

Is there anything new about this people that requires a new approach, a re-discovery, re-exploration, a re-evaluation of this subject?

Has not the church replaced the Jew and has she not been fulfilling the mission to which God called the Jews, and which they have failed to fulfill? We shall endeavor to show that this is not the case.

We shall seek to show that such a manual is vitally needed at present. 1) Because God is *not* yet through with the Jewish people and 2) because of the recent upheavals in Jewish life it appears that the books extant on this subject are not sufficiently adequate

There is much that is new about this people and much of what is old is now to be studied in a new light.

Moreover, the precarious, critical changes which mankind as a whole is now undergoing with new problems every day, new anxieties, necessitate new solutions, or rather a fresh approach, a rediscovery of old truths, and old prophecies; and the more we delve into the situation, the more we realize that we cannot just "do it" without the Jews: 1) Because they are in our midst; 2) because their history is a vital part of our civilization; 3) because of the part they are yet to play in the redemption of the world.

The world now faces an unprecedented crisis which if not overcome might soon lead the world to total destruction.

The ominous handwriting on the wall: MENE MENE TEKEL UPHARSIN (Daniel 5:25) is clearly seen by all thinking men and women; and translated into modern usage, it cautions: "A few more steps in that direction which mankind is now racing will catapult it into TOHU VABOHU — into chaos and extinction." The "heathen rage" while crying, "Peace, peace!" People, good ones and not so good ones, convene, confer, speak and write, discussing ways and means

15

of how to avert the impending catastrophe, while the "powers" whom they represent, in whose name they speak, vie with each other in accelerating the production, or acquisition, of implements for mass-annihilation.

"Peace, peace!" — but there is no peace, because the heart of man is evil: "And God saw that the wickedness of man was great in the earth, and that every imagination of the thoughts of his heart was only evil continually" (Genesis 6:5; 8:21).

Mankind is sinful and the wages of sin is death. Yet, there is a cure for man's evil heart, a remedy for his sinfulness: "the blood of Christ which taketh away the sin of the world" and its resultant evil (see John 1:29 and Hebrews 10:17). But, alas, mankind has not yet accepted this unique and only remedy. They have not yet recognized the "Prince of Peace," who for 1900 years has been calling to weary and afflicted humanity: "Come unto me, all ye that labour and are heavy laden, and I will give you rest" (Matthew 11:28). Why has mankind not availed itself of this life-saving remedy? The answer may be: Most of them have not heard of it at all, and many of them have not heard enough of it.

Was not 1900 years of grace time enough to reach the hearts of every human creature in every corner of the earth? The time, surely, was sufficient, but there were not enough true and faithful messengers to carry the Good Tidings near and far. Let us here have a swift glance at the course of the spread of the divine message: The first messengers, apostles, evangelists, were Jews, and with their typical zeal nourished by the knowledge of Christ, they launched out into the then accessible world, and not to Jews of the diaspora only, but also to Gentiles. Thousands upon thousands heard the Gospel and were convicted of its truth and its blessings. Within a relatively short period nearly all the "world," as it was known at that time, came under the sway of Christianity.

But then came a relapse. The "wild branches" which were grafted into the natural branch began to disregard and disdain the hospitality of the stem, arrogating to themselves its prerogative, deeming its life-giving sap unsavory, and even loathing its adopted parentage. Thus began the process of degeneration, deterioration and decay. Now when the "wild branches" sought to exercise their usurped authority, they exercised it with ignorance, arrogance, cruelty and failure.

For centuries the cross and the sword were almost twin brothers; at least the non-Christian nations identified them as such. It was not the Gospel of love, of the meek and "Gentle Jesus," that the Medieval Church offered and preached to those who needed it, but rather a concoction of truth and falsehood, light and darkness, allurements and threats, all mixed, and then thrust forcefully down unwilling throats.

With the Protestant Reformation there came a reformation in missionary work. The Scriptures resumed the authority which, for long years, the Catholic hierarchy had usurped. With the unadulterated Word of God in hand evangelical messengers could again carry the Gospel of love and salvation to *all* creatures.

But the endeavors were not adequate, not proportionate to the vast needs. There were not enough Christlike, self-sacrificing messengers of the Good News. And more tragic, there were even less of the love-filled, selfless messengers to bring that same Good News to the Jews next door. How well fits here: ". . . they made me the keeper of the vineyards; but mine own vineyard have I not kept" (Song of Solomon 1:6). Had they tended to their own vineyard, *the Jews* — their neighbors — first, they might have had more workers for the distant vineyards: for, every Jewish "convert" is a potential missionary and usually an extremely zealous one. As an example consider the fact that during the nineteenth century, the proportionately very little mission activity among the Jews in Europe brought about 300,000 converts. That is an enormous number, compared with the numbers of conversions in foreign lands.

Moreover, in course of time, Satan confused light with its shadow, fruit with its husks, and many of the missionaries, or mission societies, began to preach to the "benighted natives" "Christianity" rather than Christ, and that sort of "Christianity" began to be identified with "civilization" (i.e., Western civilization) with its technical achievements, schools, hospitals, museums, theaters, etc., and, to the "natives" it meant also, colonialism, conquest and subjugation to foreign masters. No wonder, that at the first opportunity, the natives, after they had learned the values of so-called "Christian civilization," made use of it in dispensing with the missionaries, in a more or less "civilized" manner. Thus, now nearly all the Gentile world is closed tightly against Christian missions.

If we were to sum up the results of 1900 years of preaching to *the Gentile "first,"* we would find that the vast majority of mankind is un-Christian, hundreds of millions are anti-Christian and most of those who are called "Christian" nations are only nominally Christian.

China, with its countless millions is now tightly closed to

Christian activities, the other Asian countries with their hundreds of millions are rapidly barring their doors to missions. The vast continent of Africa, which was once called the "*dark*" continent, is expelling the missionaries who brought them "civilization," and is now relapsing into spiritual darkness. How about Europe, the "civilized," the "Christian" continent? Recent estimates show that of the 550 million people living in Europe — 400 million have not yet heard the message of Christ. If one wants to know how many of those who *have heard* the Gospel are really followers of Christ, he may get an approximate estimate by having a look at those of the American people, for example, who "*have heard*." At present there are 66 million people in the "Christian" United States who have not any church affiliation. And those who *are* affiliated, even those who shout, "Lord, Lord," show little evidence of being regenerated. Contrasting this "Christian" complacency and indifference with the anti-Christian activities, we may have a clear picture of Satan's triumphant march, driving humanity to godlessness and destruction. The Arabs having got their education at the missionaries' schools and colleges are making enormous strides in the conquest of Afro-Asian peoples to Islam, the faith of Mohammed. Buddhism, too, has launched out to conquer the world. Competing with these are other "isms," even Rabbinism, and above all Communism, the gravest menace to humanity. All are feverishly striving to entice the world into the clutches of Satan. Thus there is confusion, ferment, turmoil, chaos — the "raging of the heathen."

Some of our liberal theologians point with satisfaction to modern society with its modern institutions and its opportunities for all, which enables the poor to live more conveniently, more luxuriously than did kings of yore, and they call this Christianity.

Is it? Probably, were it not for Christianity we might not have reached this stage of more convenient living. But this "advanced," "progressive" life with Christ left out has not made man happier, better, nobler. Had education and science been subservient to the moral values and truth of Christianity, we might enjoy their fruit, but since they became rebellious and put themselves above their mistress, their fruit has become bitter and venomous. The discoveries of the marvelous forces stored up in nature should have opened man's eyes more and more to see the omnipotence of the Creator of these forces and thus apply them only to His glory and to the welfare of His creatures. But Satan would not have permitted that. Thus the horrible abuse of the Creator's marvels. Thus also the abuse of leisure, probably the greatest blessing which technical achievement has extended to man. It is enough to scan the contents of the daily newspaper, or look and listen one evening to television, in order to be convinced that leisure is being terribly abused. Little is there, in the press as well as in television, which tends to make man better, nobler. We may assume that they provide man with what he requires. And it seems that he requires nothing more than to eat and drink and be merry, and let the morrow take care of itself!

In short, while paganism has become "civilized," "Christian civilization" has become paganized. This is what the Gentile church has achieved during 19 centuries.

WHY HAS THE CHURCH FAILED?

Why this catastrophic failure that has brought mankind to the brink of the bottomless pit?

We cannot find another answer except this: Because the "Church," however you define the word, has not obeyed the Master's injunction to "begin at Jerusalem"; it did not follow St. Paul's example to go *to the Jew first.* Mind you, both the Master's command and Apostle's example, came *after* the rejection. I stress this point "after" because there have been theologians who taught that because the Jewish people "rejected" Christ, He rejected them. They were cast away. These "modern" thoughts, and all such casuistry about God having broken His promises, abrogated His Covenant with Israel, because He is "no respecter of persons," imply that the Jews do not mean any more to Him than any other people, to say the least. All these thoughts were in vogue already in Paul's time. But Paul, who knew the Scriptures better than all theologians, past and present, who knew, loved and obeyed his Master more than they have done, emphatically refuted them: assuring and reassuring those that wanted to know, that God does not change, that Israel is still His "Chosen people," and it is still *to the Jew first.* No, He is not through with them; He still has a great future in store for them, and He still wants them to carry out their mission to all mankind. (See Romans 3:1-2 and chapter 11.)

How those old doubts, heresies and prejudices, persisted all through the nineteenth centuries; how modernists still try to twist and squeeze out of a certain word or words, culled out of their context from the Scriptures, "proofs" that they are right, and not

Jesus and not Paul, is hard to comprehend. It only shows how powerful Satan is to confuse man's mind and lead him astray.

Again and again we hear the argument: "The Jews had their chance and failed it, so the 'Church' assumed their mission." Now, we might similarly contend: "The 'Church' has had its chance and failed, so perhaps we'd better go back to the Jews."

But why use childish arguments, when the Bible from Genesis to Revelation revolves around this Jewish people? Those that would "cast away" this people, would do well if they first cast away the entire Bible.

After the Bible has related the fall of mankind, it goes on relating the history of the people whom God chose to lift it up again. For many generations the Lord led this people through rigorous training and education. From time to time He manifested His will and instructions to them in diverse manners; sometimes it was through the Holy Spirit by the prophets, sometimes by personal revelation, and finally with the climax when the Word became flesh. All theophanies had the one purpose, to prepare and equip this people for the universal ministry (a "kingdom of ministers") of proclaiming to all nations the glory of God and the saving grace which is in the supreme sacrifice of His only Son for the atonement of their sins. The Jewish people is still God's witness, whether they, themselves, or their antagonists like it or not. Their tragic history serves as incontestable proof that the Bible is the Word of God and that He cares for the salvation of mankind. At present, the Jew may be His unwilling witness, but the time will come when he will become a willing and most efficient witness.

Why did the Jews, as a people, reject the Messiah, whom they so anxiously expected? Was God's choice of this people wrong? Was all His training and disciplining then a failure?

These are blasphemous questions — silly, childish questions. But strange as it is, there are mature people, even learned people who, by their talk, evoke such speculations. It is quite *natural*. Man, who takes pride in his wisdom and logical thinking, presumes to measure and weigh God's wisdom and deeds according to his own standards. We do not know what might have been the course of history had *not* blindness in part afflicted the Jewish people; had they not stumbled; had they accepted their Messiah when He came to them. We do not know what might have been, but we *do* know, that whatever happened, happened according to God's plans. To us, to mortal man, it is a mystery. Yet, Paul, inspired by God, instructs us and comforts us: "For I would not, brethren, that ye should be ignorant of this mystery, lest ye should be wise in your own conceits; that blindness in part is happened to Israel, until the fulness of the Gentiles be come in" (Romans 11:25); and his chapter 11 to the Romans, if we read it prayerfully, will shed heavenly light on the matter and reveal to us at least part of this mystery. However, the Lord Himself told His faithful disciples, at their first meeting after His death, that it was not for them to know God's times and seasons. For them, as for all other believers, it is *only* to be His witnesses — and *to begin at Jerusalem* (Luke 24:47 and Acts 1:6-8). In short, as regards the evangelization of the Jews, as indeed in all other human conduct, we are bound to subjugate our wills to God's will; we are to obey His command implicitly and leave His planning and the results to Him.

Yet I shall try to give a reply to some questions which I have been. asked lately:

1. Are the Jews now more than before spiritually prepared for this vital change of heart and mind; to return to the God of the Sacred Scriptures, find out what is His will and fulfill it?

2. Are they now, more than before, physically and mentally equipped with the necessary qualifications for their mission?

3. Are they now more than before willing to take upon themselves this most difficult and hazardous task?

To question No. 1 our reply is "Yes." For the first time in Jewish history the Jews are beginning to ask, "What is Judaism?" During the time of the prophets there was the question, whether to serve Baal, or Jehovah, or both. When it became clear that Jehovah God was the only One, Judaism then meant to serve Him in accordance with His commandments as recorded in the Sacred Scriptures. With the coming of the Messiah Jesus a crisis came which changed the whole course of Jewish history. While thousands of Jews believed in Christ, the people as a whole followed their leaders who rejected Him and His teaching.

Soon afterward, Jerusalem, including the Holy Temple, the center of Judaism, was destroyed and its people was dispersed into many lands. Now again large numbers of Jews came to know Jesus and followed Him. But the people, as a whole, blindly followed those rabbis who promised that if they would keep the Torah, observe its commandments scrupulously and conscientiously, God would send them the Messiah who would return them to the

Promised Land and to pristine glory. But how could they keep God's commands when almost all of them were, directly or indirectly, connected with and dependent upon the sacrificial ordinances which could not be observed when there was no Temple and no altar?

Were the leaders at that time not stricken with partial blindness, they would have seen that their Redeemer liveth — that He was the living, the only sacrifice. As it was, they salvaged the few commands which could be kept even in exile and built around them "hedges" and "fences," as they called it, till the original Judaism became distorted beyond recognition.

The leaders cherished the hope that this mode of Judaism would serve the people as a vessel to carry them on the seas of exile safely till the Messiah would come. Thus they embarked in a wreck on the boisterous, uncharted seas with raging billows pounding on it, with pilots who knew little of navigation. Countless were their losses, indescribable their suffering, as they were tossed about during the nineteen centuries of exile. Yet, they patiently endured their trials and tribulations in the assurance that the Messiah and their deliverance might come at any moment. All they had to do to be worthy and to hasten His coming was to observe meticulously, implicitly, all the laws and ordinances which the rabbis had "prescribed." This they did, zealously and unswervingly, doing all that the rabbis enjoined them to do. This implicit faith in the rabbis and their type of Judaism could thrive only under the strict surveillance and constant watch of the rabbis and was made possible when the Jews in the diaspora lived segregated in ghettos, depending on each other, responsible for each other, in a hostile menacing world around them, where the synagogue was the center of life, where all "foreign" (Gentile) ideas were anathema, where no book besides the rabbinic books could penetrate. That was "Judaism," the Judaism of the exile, the Judaism of the ghetto. But the old Ghetto walls now have crumbled and collapsed beyond repair.

There came the age of "Enlightenment," the age of "Emancipation," and enlightened and emancipated Jews began to think for themselves. They began to doubt the wisdom of the rabbis and to wonder whether the words of Isaiah of old were not meant also for later ages: ". . . O my people, they which lead thee cause thee to err, and destroy the way of thy paths" (Isaiah 3:12). New leaders arose, various "isms" were initiated to replace that so-called "Judaism" which was rapidly deteriorating and disintegrating. But all "isms," all new hopes and aspirations were shattered during the last score of years. All the hopes and dreams that modern "emancipated" Jews had conceived in regard to education, progress, science, democracy, socialism and the like, vanished during the years of World War II, the Nazi atrocities, and the bankruptcy of Communism, as an ideal.[1]

The establishment of the State of Israel brought some new hope to weary and heavy-laden Jewries all over the diaspora. But it was also the new "State" that challenged traditional "Judaism" to reality, to life in a modern State. It was there, in the new State of Israel, that the question arose, "What is Judaism?"

The rabbis have not yet relinquished their hope of reinstating their brand of Judaism. Imposing synagogues are being erected, various attractions and inducements are offered to enlist members; much is done to make Judaism more attractive, more palatable, more digestible. But all in vain. The people as a whole stand now at the cross-roads, disillusioned and confused, and ask: "Whither?"

The answer to their quandary we are to supply. "Whither?" they ask: The answer is, we should say: " 'Return ye, all the way back to your God, who has chosen you to be His holy people and to make Him known to all the peoples of the earth.' It is to that end, that God has preserved you through all those vicissitudes." The survival of the Jewish people in a world alien and hostile to them, is the greatest mystery and miracle in the history of mankind. The Jews know that. They also know that they were destined by God to make Him known to all the world. Even their liberals and agnostics acknowledge this, although it is all quite hazy to them. They know that they have not yet carried out this worldwide mission. Why? Because, having followed false prophets and blind leaders their knowledge of God, His Word and His will, became muddled and adulterated. The highest, noblest ideals were exchanged for the observances of meaningless rites, which could never have appealed to the hearts of the Gentile world; nor could they have satisfied their own longings. Least of all could these petty rites, which have become known as "Judaism," have given a man the assurance that he is one with God, that his sins have been atoned for.

This kind of Judaism now has less appeal than ever to other peoples because most Jews themselves have abandoned it. They

[1] See chapter, "A Peculiar People; A Glance at Their History."

themselves realize that it is not leading them in the right direction
— back to the God of their fathers.[2]

It is thus our task to show them the way back to God who
revealed Himself to their ancestors and by whose everlasting
covenant *all the families of the earth* were to be blessed (Genesis
12:3); we are to show them that all subsequent revelations confirmed this covenant and its divine purpose.

2. Are they now, more than before, physically and mentally
equipped with the necessary qualifications for their mission? Here,
too, the answer is "Yes." Already in the time of Christ the Jewish
people were well prepared for their mission to a world sunk in
the mire of idolatry, sin and corruption. They had the Word of
God, they loved it and were ready to guard and defend it with
their very lives. They had a fair knowledge of the nations around
them with whom they traded and among whom they had settled
in large numbers. They had the message and they had the means
of communicating with other people. Some, like Paul and the
other disciples, fulfilled the mission excellently, but the people
as a whole failed.

Since that time the Jewish people has had additional training,
not by direct revelation, through prophets, but indirectly by harsh
experience. It was a post graduate course, each lesson beaten in
by hard blows. Now, after 1900 years of rigorous schooling, they
have learned to know all nations and to live with them; they have
learned to endure all climates, to overcome difficulties which to
other people would be insurmountable. This schooling in exile, has
equipped them with exceptional intellectual endowments in such
qualities as perseverance, resourcefulness and initiative, with am-
bition and energy. Proof: After about 1900 years of economic and
social restrictions, severe degradation, oppressive laws and legal
disabilities, and in spite of hate and prejudice with its periodic
outbursts of mob violence, massacres, gas-chambers and concentra-
tion camps, they have survived. One may now encounter them
in the highest positions of human civilization. They are to be
found high up in industry and commerce, in finance, law, and medicine and in all branches of art, science and in politics. What is most
important, they can and do create and shape moral ideas and
public opinion since they exert such an influence on the press,
theatre, radio, television and education.

These high intellectual endowments can be used for good

2 See chapter on Sects.

or abused for evil; they can make or break, do or undo, kill or cure. Generally, the Jews have used their abilities for self-defense and for self-perpetuation. Their extraordinary potentialities are well demonstrated in the upbuilding of the new State of Israel where, within a few years, they have turned a barren desert into a flourishing land, and that with almost no implements and no previous experience. And these gifts were bestowed on them not only for their own good, but for the good of all mankind — "All the families of the earth" are to be blessed through them. Yes, the Jews are more than ever before, qualified to accomplish the task which was given to them by God from the time of Abraham.

3. Are they now more willing to take upon themselves this most difficult, hazardous task? Again the answer is "Yes." However, we should bear in mind that no man has ever been too willing to undertake a task which is likely to incur great suffering and expose him to ridicule, hate and persecution. Moses, greatest of prophets, hesitated persistently before he obeyed God's command to go to Pharaoh. The other prophets, too, tried to evade God when He ordered them on difficult missions. Even the Saviour Himself, in the flesh, pleaded, "O my Father, if it be possible, let this cup pass from me: nevertheless not as I will, but as thou wilt" (Matthew 26:39).

The Jews have always been a zealous people. They have been the most idealistic people on earth. They have always been in search of the highest ideals, and when they found one which they thought was the right one, they devoted all their heart and mind to it. No other nation has had so many martyrs as they have had. They have always been ready to offer on the altar of their faith not only their possessions but also their very life. They showed the same ardor, enthusiasm and self-sacrifice, when one or another "ism" captured their heart as a great "ideal."

Now that they have come to realize that the zeal with which they had hitherto worshiped God, has been without knowledge: and now that they have become disillusioned with the various "isms," which they believed would bring salvation to mankind, they ought surely to be ready to give their all to the one and only ideal of salvation for Jew and Gentile alike when the knowledge of this ideal is impressed upon their hearts. And their hearts have never been more open for it.

It is thus the purpose of this book to assist every Christian in finding the way to the Jewish heart, and the prerequisite to reach man's heart is love. But one cannot really love what one does not know.

There is a fourth question which we have been asked: Are there not enough books on Judaism, why one more? My answer is: Yes, there are plenty of books, more elegant, more scholarly than I may boast for mine, but they lack a necessary perspective which this book will emphasize. As I point out in the Chapter on "The Jewish Religion," most, if not all, of those books have, it seems, only one aim: to glorify Judaism and show its superiority over Christianity, thus only what fits into that frame is used and what does not well fit in is ignored.

How I Came to Write This Book

I became aware of the need of such a special presentation for Christians years ago soon after the Lord had called me to dedicate my life to the evangelization of my people. I had my own struggle at "Peniel," as did my forefather Jacob, but the "Angel of the Lord" blessed me and promised to be with me and guide me through all the difficulties encountered in such a mission.

· When I began my practical work, I realized that the old methods of reaching the Jews through mission centers was not sufficient. There were more than 6,000,000 Jews in the United States scattered in over 9,000 cities and towns. A large army of qualified missionaries and hundreds of centers would be needed to reach them.

I therefore saw no other solution to this problem than to place the responsibility for evangelizing the Jews primarily at the door of the local churches by challenging each church to minister to the Jews of their vicinity. We have a good example of the effectiveness of this in the early church. The apostles sowed the seed which fell on fertile ground, producing rich friut. This fruit was disseminated and in turn produced more fruit and so on. Every one of the followers became a missionary, which explains the rapid growth of the early church.

I wish to say, however, that I do not desire to minimize the efforts put forth by mission centers. They have their place in large cities as well as in foreign countries and have rendered monumental service. Without them the fires of Jewish evangelism might long ago have been extinguished.

This conviction I have voiced by word of mouth from thousands of pulpits as well as through the printed page, and, thank God, the appeal has not been without effect. The response was heart-warming. Requests for advice and instruction began to pour in from earnest Christians who realized that they were duty bound to make Christ known to their Jewish friends but they did not know how to approach them, for they knew as little about the inner life of the Jewish people within their gates as they did about the peoples in distant lands.

Here is a letter typical of the requests which we received at that time:

> Very often I have felt guilty of negligence of the divine command, "To the Jew first," and I have tried to calm my conscience with the thought that the Jews did have the Gospel first and re-jected it and that the command is no longer binding upon Christians today. But your message enlightened me very much and I realize now that it is the duty of every follower of Christ to carry the Gospel "To the Jew first."
>
> However, like many others, I feel so inadequate in contacting my Jewish friends, and should like to know more about them, their relationship to Christianity, how to approach them, how to gain their confidence, how to win them to Christ. I feel that from your many years of experience in preaching the Gospel to your own people, you would have valuable advice to offer. So please (and I am sure that many others join me in this plea) take the time to prepare a manual on the subject.

Requests in such a spirit, both oral and written, have been received from hundreds of devout Christians and I am sure that there are thousands who would welcome something to guide and direct them in their witnessing to the Jew.

The great need for information on the real life of the Jewish people has been recognized not only by the layman but also by Christian leaders and missionary organizations, as the following transcript shows:

Dr. C. E. Matthews, Director of Evangelism under the Home Mission Board of the Southern Baptist Convention, requested me to write a chapter for his book, *The Southern Baptist Program for Evangelism.* In his preface to that chapter he writes:

> It is the writer's belief that of all minority groups the most neglected by Christians in soul-winning is the Jew. . . . The writer himself is very guilty of this sin of neglect. Ninety-nine times out of a hundred we, as Christians, will pass by the Jew and seek to win the Gentile in evangelism. We make no plans

to win the Jew and apparently, from the amount of praying we do in their behalf, we reveal our utter lack of interest in the spiritual welfare of the people who Paul said were to have first access to the Gospel and over whom our Saviour bitterly wept because of their spiritual blindness. The first concern in the heart of Paul was for the Jew. So deep was his concern and so great was his pity and love for them that he cried with bitter tears for three years as he pleaded day and night with them. We are trying to work out a plan in our program of evangelism to attract the Jew to the preaching of the Gospel and to include him in our efforts to win a lost world to Jesus.

One of the main reasons that Gentile Christians hesitate to try to win Jews to Christ is that we are ignorant concerning their many and varied religious sects in Bible times and now and concerning what each of them believes. For this reason we have asked Dr. Jacob Gartenhaus, Secretary of the Department of Jewish Evangelism of the Home Mission Board, to write an article on the subject of evangelizing the Jew. Dr. Gartenhaus has favored us with an article on the subject written especially for this book. In this article we have found more actual information on the subject than we have ever read in any book outside of the Bible.

But articles in newspapers and magazines were not enough: they might easily be overlooked. So in response to many further requests, I published my first tract, *How to Win the Jews*. So great was the demand for it that I had to reprint it again and again, altogether in 22 editions — almost half a million copies.

This small tract, however, became inadequate after the Second World War. Things have changed enormously. A new world emerged from the debris of the old, and the greatest change of all occurred within the Jewish people. The horrible German atrocities which were climaxed in the slaughter of about 6,000,000 Jews while the civilized world looked calmly on without any serious protest, had such a disillusioning effect upon the lives of those who survived that they despaired of ever being able to expect anything but trouble from non-Jews.

Yet mightier than these negative causes for the changes in Jewish life, and its relation to the non-Jewish world, was the positive cause of the establishment of the national home — the State of Israel. The Jew no longer felt himself to be a homeless creature wandering from one place to another where sooner or later he would again become an object of hate, persecution and expulsion. He had become conscious of the fact that now he had a haven where he would be welcomed as a brother and fellow citizen. Indeed, the Jew has become a sound, normal, human being with but little of the complexes and problems that were the marks of the wandering Jew — the ghetto Jew.

We became aware of the fact that the Jewish people is in the process of being remodelled, recast; the dry bones of Israel are coming to life, a new type of Jew is now being born. Christians everywhere know that a miracle is happening before their eyes: ancient prophecies are being fulfilled and now more than ever they want to know this wonder-nation — the peculiar people.

Thus in response to the recent urgent requests we are now publishing a new and much enlarged guide to "win the Jew." Our earnest prayer and sincere hope is that this book may lead its readers to the knowledge and the love which is required in approaching the Jew and winning his heart to his true Messiah.

Chapter II

A PECULIAR PEOPLE

A Glance at Their Singularity

Some words of caution:

In all your dealings with the Jew, remember that, although he affirms that he wants to be treated like any other human being, he was, is and will ever be aware of being a peculiar people. His first patriarch Abraham was peculiar, was different from all men around him. And God chose him and his descendants to be His people, holy, separate, and exemplary. When Jacob came to Egypt he asked for and received a separated, exclusive place for settlement. For hundreds of years Jacob's offspring (the Jews) lived in Egypt and remained a distant people. Egyptian civilization with its few virtues and many vices had no effect on them. Balaam saw their camp in the desert and prophesied their future as "a people that shall dwell alone and among the nations it shall not be reckoned" (Numbers 23:9).

The Law on Sinai, by inculcating into their hearts and minds the faith in the One True God, and the abhorrence of any other gods, was the final touch (the master stroke) which separated them forever from all other people.

For many years there were several attempts by the Jews to be like other people, but God always frustrated such attempts. "And that which cometh into your mind shall not be at all, that ye say, We will be as the heathen, as the families of the countries, to serve wood and stone" (Ezekiel 20:32).

During their first exile in Babylon large numbers of Jews became "like others." They assimilated and vanished as Jews, but the main stem remained intact. Many of them returned to Zion, where they could live apart from Gentile contact and influence.

During the period of the second Temple many Jews tried to be like the Greeks, then like the Romans, but the nation as a whole preserved its integrity. After centuries of vigorous training by the prophets and their successors, the Jews, by the time of their second exile, were already thoroughly imbued with what we call Judaism. Nothing could turn them from it and it involved a life peculiar, distinct, and isolated from the life of all other people.

It often happened that, in order to escape persecution, or to gain recognition when needed, Jews found it necessary to assume "Gentilism," to put on Gentile garb and to speak Gentile language. Sometimes even to shave the beard and the sidelocks in order to look like a "goy." After living in a country long enough to be acclimated and adapted to environment, they even began to look like their Gentile neighbors, like Arabs in Arabia, like Chinese in China, like Germans in Germany, etc.

But all adaptations and simulations were only external. Essentially the Jew remained Jewish no matter what disguise he put on. There has always been the almost impregnable wall of partition between Jew and Gentile. No matter what contacts he made with the Gentile outside, his home always remained the sanctuary of Judaism whereto the Gentiles had no access, except occasionally for some business transaction. They could not dine together. There could be no thought of intermarriage. There was no particular subject which could be equally near and dear to both of them. The usual subjects of the Jew's conversation have been Judaism and the Jewish people at home and abroad, in all corners of the earth. Of course he could not share his feelings about these with his Gentile friends. Nor could he share such sentiments· as the Gentile is likely to voice. What is dear to the Gentile (especially religion) has always been, at best, taboo to the Jew. The practices and rites of non-Jewish religions whether Egyptian, Babylonian, Canaanite, Greek, Roman, so sacred, so dear to his Gentile neighbor, were an abomination to the Jews. And so were the rites, processions and pomp of medieval Christianity. The bloody sports and pastimes of Spain, fencing in Germany and prize fights in America, etc., have, to the Jew, been equally brutal, unfit for man created in the image of God. Nor have the carnivals, the various races, masquerades, dance parties ever been to his liking. The average Jew cannot fathom why a man should be so enthusiastic, so excited, so engrossed in physical sports as is the average Gentile.

Not only have these differences kept the Jew apart from the Gentile, he has also distrusted the Gentile, considering him unpredictable and unstable, who might get drunk (or be incited by some demagogue) and start a quarrel which could lead to a general brawl and bloodshed. So he has stood apart and aloof, looking down upon the Gentile as an inferior being. Every day in prayer the pious Jew thanks God for not having made him a Gentile. While this self-righteousness is not praiseworthy we may admit that the average Jew has in most cases stood above his Gentile environment in moral virtues. In all places at all times he was more humane than those around him. Why so? Because at all times and in all places he took the Scriptures as his guide. Not always did he interpret God's Word properly, and not always did he follow His guidance. There were times when he would sacrifice his life for every iota; there were times when his zeal was without knowledge; there were times as in the present when he was ready to abandon the precepts of the Torah — but always he was proud of his heritage, proud of being peculiar, and proudly conscious of the obligation to be better than the "goyim." Noblesse oblige: He being of noble ancestry.

That they survived notwithstanding all the vicissitudes to which they were exposed in dispersion among hostile peoples, proves that their aloofness, their being peculiar, has been justified, has been of God.

A. The Peculiar Nature of Work Among the Peculiar People

To be an ambassador of God and particularly to the Jews is the greatest privilege which a human being may attain. But this also involves great responsibility, devotion, spiritual fortitude, an abundance of love and patience, and last but not least a fair knowledge of this extraordinary people.

Remember, the approach to the Jew must be altogether different from that to any other people. The African tribesman, for example, having no deep-rooted prejudices against Christ or Christianity, may after some hesitation cautiously try to get acquainted with the missionary and listen to what he has to tell him.

Things have radically changed everywhere in recent years. The "natives" no longer fear or revere the "white man." Up until a few years ago they considered the white missionary as a member of the superman race, possessor of extraordinary might, wisdom and wealth, who would dispense to them money, food, clothing, medicine, education and other advantages that make the white man great, if they (the natives) would accept the white man's God.

It is not so with the Jew. He is quite satisfied with himself. He is sure that the missionary has nothing to offer him except a religion which his teachers have taught him to abhor, to despise, to shun. He has always been conscious of being the elite, and above all other nations, an aristocrat whose noble lineage goes back thousands of years, who possessed the highest degree of true culture long before the nascence of the people who now are so boastful of their civilization. He has always been firmly convinced that his people are the wisest of people and that he is superior to all other nations in noble virtues, such as purity of mind and body, sobriety, charity, etc. Prejudice, fortified with some experience, has taught him that he has nothing to gain by abandoning Judaism and going over to "another religion," but on the contrary, he has everything to lose. "Judaism" is not just a belief in certain doctrines or a performance of certain rites (on special occasions) but it is his very life and being. We shall see later in the chapter on Sects, that even the present-day Jew who is slack in the observance of the traditional laws and customs still feels as one with those of past generations who zealously clung to those laws and customs. "Going over" to Christianity is considered by *all* Jews (observant or non-observant) as desertion to the enemy's camp, as high treason, as an unpardonable sin.

Furthermore, whereas the Gentile after having become Christian may often remain with his kinfolks as peacefully and amicably as before, the Jew, on becoming a Christian, might immediately and cruelly be ostracized from his people; his parents would lament him as dead and curse his memory, and his friends would turn to be his implacable adversaries. In short, he would become an outcast and everything would be done to make his life miserable.

There surely are discouragements and inconveniences in evangelizing the Jew, but there are also a great many advantages in this particular field which outweigh all the disadvantages (and which one does not find in other fields).

In the Jew, contrary to the foreign "native," you will find generally an intelligent, clean and sober person with whom you as a Christian have much in common. You may discuss with him politics, economics, social and civic affairs and often also literature, music and art, etc., which may be of interest to both of you. And above all, there is the Bible (in this case the Old Testament) which is regarded as holy by both of you. Moreover, the subject of Christianity is not foreign to him although much of his knowledge about it is badly distorted.

Furthermore there is that great advantage in "converting" a Jew, in that one may have the assurance of not only having saved a precious soul, but of having also given birth to a new missionary. It is, as we have shown, difficult to convince the Jew that his conception and evaluation of Christ and Christianity has been wrong. But as soon as he is convinced of his error, and his ignorance turns into knowledge, there is no holding him back from rushing out and calling, "Eureka, I have found it!" First he wants to exculpate, exonerate himself before his people by proving why he has accepted Jesus as his Messiah. By so doing he is a missionary indirectly. Then, as his self-defense is usually of no avail, because his people will always think of him as an apostate, a renegade, or at best a demented character, he usually takes to the direct mission work to show his people that not only is he not to be blamed for his acceptance of the Messiah, but rather he ought to be emulated by all his people, since Jesus the Messiah is the only Way, the Truth, and the Life, and that in following Him, one fulfills the true Jewish faith, becomes a completed Jew.

And he is well equipped for his mission work, because it took him a long time of arduous study, inquiries and arguments before he finally was sure that Jesus is not only his personal Saviour but also national Messiah and the only hope for his people.

But whether Jewish mission work is difficult or not, whether it is pleasant or not, advantageous or not, we must remember that we are on marching orders and we are not to argue with our Superior on High. Our Sovereign who commissioned us is not paying us a prize for each and every soul we bring to Him. Our orders are to preach, to sow the seed. The results of our preaching and sowing are in the hand of God, not in our hand. (Even if our seed has fallen on barren rocks we have done well because we have carried out His orders.) And we must bear in mind that God's commission is not to be trifled with. (See Ezekiel, chapters two and three.) "Son of man, I have made thee a watchman unto the house of Israel: therefore hear the word at my mouth, and give them warning from me. When I say unto the wicked, Thou shalt surely die; and thou givest him not warning, nor speakest to warn the wicked from his wicked way, to save his life; the same wicked man shall die in his iniquity; but his blood will I require at thine hand. Yet if thou warn the wicked, and he turn not from his wickedness, nor from his wicked way, he shall die in his iniquity; but thou hast delivered thy soul. Again, When a righteous man doth turn from his righteousness, and commit iniquity, and I lay a stumbling block before him, he shall die: because thou hast not given him warning, he shall die in his sin, and his righteousness which he hath done shall not be remembered; but his blood will I require at thine hand. Nevertheless if thou warn the righteous man, that the righteous sin not, and he doth not sin, he shall surely live, because he is warned; also thou hast delivered thy soul" (Ezekiel 3:17-21). On the other hand, we are entitled to expect visible success of our faithful labor as the Psalmist assures us: "They that sow in tears shall reap in joy" (Psalm 126:5).

Yet, just as we ought to know the kind of field we are about to cultivate, we ought to know how to plow and harrow it, find the opportune time for sowing the seed, etc., we ought to have a knowledge of the Jewish field, and it is our hope and prayer that this book will provide this knowledge.

Hence let us get better acquainted with the present-day Jew and his background. This book is not going to tell you "all about the Jews." Many large volumes could not do that. Our intention is to open a window through which you may have a glimpse of the life of this unique people. You'll have to widen the view, to see more and more of it, from every angle. We thus hope that this book will spur you on to further, deeper study of the Jew's history, the longest and the most interesting history of any nation, of his literature, the richest of any nation, and of his religious life, the most devoted life of any nation.

The more you learn to know this peculiar people, the more you will understand the Holy Scriptures, the more you will grasp why God has chosen this people, and to what sublime purpose. And, last but not least, you will better understand the New Testament people — all Jews — their thoughts, their actions.

B. A GLANCE AT JEWISH HISTORY

The history of the Jewish people is the most eventful, the most colorful, the most tragic history of any other people past or present. It is a most spell-binding, entrancing story of narrow escapes, of miracles, real miracles, and you would do well to acquire a fair knowledge of it. Without the knowledge of his long, most eventful history as background, you would know little of the present day Jew.

Jewish history is composed of two parts: 1. The Bible which is the history of the Jews from the very beginning until after their return from the Babylonian exile. The Apocrypha (especially the book of the Maccabees) and the New Testament books reveal a great part of their life during the Second Commonwealth. 2. Post-biblical history.

But, bear in mind that while the Bible is an inspired, holy book, the later history books are to be taken critically, with a "grain of salt." The Bible, although written by Jews, is no respecter of persons. When something was wrong with the Jews or with their leaders the Bible records it truthfully in unequivocal words. Sometimes it even appeared that the authors were too severe, too exacting, too censorious in regard to their people. It is not so with the later histories in which one will not find much fault with the Jews. If anything went wrong among Jewry it was almost always someone else (the "goy") who was to be blamed. As regards the relations between Jews and the Gentile world, the Jewish nation is pictured as an innocent lamb among seventy wolves. (In Jewish tradition the Gentile world is composed of seventy nations.)

This conception of Jewish self-righteousness all through the exile is to a large extent justifiable. If the Jews ever were mercenary, parsimonious, usurious, tricky, with which they often have been charged, they were forced to it by their adversaries. It was a matter of self-defense and survival; but whatever they were, they never were worse than their enemies and accusers, and often not as bad.

Their life in exile was one continuous struggle for survival. And whereas they did survive, it proves either that they are the fittest people on earth, according to "modern" theories or evolution, or, as we believe, God has preserved them miraculously for some purpose which we well know.

C. Who Is a Jew?

Now we have spoken of the "Jew" taking it for granted that you know who is a Jew. To a certain extent you do. Everyone "knows" who is a "Jew"; and yet, Jews themselves have lately raised the question, "Who is a Jew?"

It was in the new State of Israel where there arose the demand for an answer to this question. And the answer to "Who is a Jew?" is now being discussed with much concern and acerbity by the Jews all over the world. So you see that even among the Jews themselves there is no consensus as to "Who is a Jew?" Some say that only he who observes the laws of "Judaism" or rather "Rabbinism" is a Jew, whether of Jewish or Gentile descent. Others say that the observance of religion does not matter; it is only race which makes one a Jew. And there are various modifications of these two opinions.

Judaism has undergone various radical changes during the

ages. One of the greatest changes, as previously mentioned, transpired during the eighteenth century when the Jews in Western Europe were enfranchised. Availing themselves of the rights to citizenship most of them left their ghettos with the intent to become knitted into one nation with the people of the country in which they sojourned. Gradually they abandoned all their own laws and customs that served to keep them apart from their Gentile neighbors, retaining but a few non-essential customs to be observed as a sort of "Judaism."

During this eighteenth century, while thousands abandoned traditional Judaism, straying into agnosticism and other "isms," about 300,000 Jews in Western countries accepted Christianity as their religion. So it was wherever their neighbors were Christian enough to show them a good example of what Christianity really is.

If the Jewish communities in these "free" countries did not totally disappear, it is due mostly to the repeated infusions of Judaism by the influx of Jewish immigrants who came from Eastern Europe (Russia, Poland, Rumania and others). There the Jews remained disqualified for citizenship. There they remained in their ghettos apart from the Gentiles outside the ghetto walls. There they were left to themselves, and traditional Judaism remained the greatest factor of Jewish life — the most precious treasure worth keeping and living for. As these poverty-stricken habitations became more and more overcrowded, many had to depart and "go West" in the hope of finding their fortune abroad. These were the wanderers who instilled some new life into the dry bones of Western Jewry.

Thus the Jews of East European countries have for many generations served as a reservoir of traditional Judaism from whose constant overflow, their Western brethren who living in freedom were inclined to assimilate and be absorbed among the non-Jewish population, were somewhat restrained and resuscitated. They retained some semblance of Judaism making concessions to modern life and environment.

Then came that great catastrophe which practically wiped out "Eastern" Jewry, which had so long served as the mainspring and mainstay of Judaism.

First came the Nazi German horrible onslaught which exterminated about six million of those Jews — the majority of European Jewry. Then came Russian Communism which cruelly suppressed all vestiges of Judaism, thus forcing the three million Jews living under its sway to dissociate from their brethren abroad and assimilate and disappear as a people.

This double catastrophe was potent enough to instill despair into Jewish hearts all over the world and incline them to give up the struggle for remaining "Jewish." But God does not want the Jewish people to despair and disappear. A new star of hope rose on their horizon, twinkling and auguring new life and a glorious future: It was the establishment of the "State of Israel."

D. THE STATE OF ISRAEL AS FACTOR OF NEW TRENDS IN JUDAISM

The State of Israel was to serve not only as a place of refuge, a haven of rest for all Jews who could not and would not stay in exile, that is, in Gentile lands, but also as a center of Jewish culture and religion which would shine as a beacon light to Jewry all over the world. It was to be a paradigm of how to live as Jews, and as the prophets envisaged it long ago; from Zion would come forth the Law, and the Word of God from Jerusalem (see Isaiah 2:3). It was hoped that there would be established (reinstituted) a supreme authority like the Men of the Great Synagogue or the later "Sanhedrin" who would judge and decide on all matters pertaining to Judaism. This hope is suffering much disappointment and setback because most rabbis, especially in the diaspora, tenaciously hold to their medieval tenet that "Judaism" means all the laws and customs introduced into Jewish life throughout the ages. And this is the type of Judaism they want to perpetuate in Israel. Behind these rabbis stand most of the Jews in the diaspora, who themselves are very lax in observing the innumerable rabbinic laws, but who expect their brethren living in Israel to do so. To them it is a kind of proxy religion, as if to say, and some say it expressly, "We of the diaspora provide the funds to preserve your State so that you in turn preserve our religion — with which we cannot be bothered here. We pay and you pray."

But the great majority of Israeli Jews who for the first time in the last nineteen centuries have tasted freedom, do not like to be fettered and enslaved again by any people, including the rabbis. Moreover, most of the Jews who settled in Israel since the establishment of the Jewish State have previously been weaned away from traditional "Judaism," as have most Jews in the Western world.

---

[1] A body of authorized rabbis sitting in the "seat of Moses" as ordained in Deuteronomy 17:8-13 and acknowledged by Jesus (Matthew 23:2). According to tradition it was instituted by Ezra and Nehemiah.

However, the greatest obstacle to "Judaism" as the rabbis understand it and strive to enforce it, is the "State" itself, or rather, the life in a modern state. For example, the observance of the rabbinic laws governing Sabbath rest would paralyze all modern communication and transportation, and cause untold trouble to the individual inhabitants of Israel, as well as grave danger to the security of the State as a whole. The same may be said about many other rabbinic laws which might endanger the functions of the State and the welfare of its inhabitants.

But whatever the temporary differences, difficulties and perplexities, the Jewish people tenaciously hold on to the great hope and ideal of Zion becoming not only the religious center of the Jewish people, but also becoming a "Light to the Nations." How will this hope materialize? Many still believe that the Messiah will soon come and establish the glorious "Messianic Age." Others are skeptical; many disbelieve in supernatural changes. Yet the "State of Israel" as the rock upon which will be established the salvation of Israel, and by it, the whole world, is the hope, the only hope which now keeps the Jews and Judaism alive.

Our next chapter on Types and Segments will present a closer view of present-day Jewry in its diversities and in its unity as a whole.

CHAPTER III

TYPES AND SEGMENTS

After some initial talk with a Jew, you will soon discover what type of Jew he is; whether he is learned in Jewish lore, or in general knowledge, or if he is ignorant in one or in both, and you will have to deal with him accordingly.

With the intellectual, well-informed Jew you may cite Scriptures, hold a theological, philosophical discourse. He will easily understand what you will have to say; he probably harbors in his heart less prejudice; he no longer believes the puerile fairy tales that were circulated within the walls of the ghetto about Jesus. But he may also be better equipped to dispute and to argue against your views. In him you have a well-armed opponent.

But with the uninformed and ignorant as far as religion is concerned — and there are many Jews who know little about Judaism and less about Christianity — you have to deal quite differently. The great majority of Jews today belong to this type. All they may know about Jesus and His teaching is a collection of grotesque tales, and all that they have heard of Christianity is a distortion of facts or outright falsehoods. You will *first* have to disprove his erroneous conceptions, and that should not be a hard task. (See Chapter on "Some Practical Ways of Approach.") *Then* you will show him (as is the case with all Jews) that his faith in those leaders who condemned Jesus may have been wrong, unjustified. You might have to prove that others of the Jewish leaders have erred[1], and often the whole people has erred also. They almost stoned Moses, they persecuted the greatest of the prophets, etc. *Finally* you will show him that he (like you) and everyone else, is a sinner and in need of pardon, and that there is no pardon except by Jesus. From this stage on, your whole dealings with him will be on that point (sin and salvation) which we will discuss later on.

After your introductory conversation, you will have discovered

[1] "O my people, they which lead thee cause thee to err, and destroy the way of thy paths" (Isaiah 3:12).

what are his religious convictions, what are his views on Judaism in general, and you may deal with him accordingly.

THE AVERAGE JEW
The Spiritual Heir to Traditional Judaism

The various views which the Jews of the present day hold about their religion (Judaism), are not now so marked and clearly defined as they were two to three generations ago. Then the various segments of Jewry often fought bitterly with one another in defense of their particular convictions. *Today there are not many Jews who are ready for a serious wrangle in order to defend and enforce their own views and opinions. Doubt and skepticism are gravely undermining old beliefs. Religious disputes are now regarded as petty bickerings, fighting windmills and shadows.* What the Jews, in general, want now is the survival of the nation. They feel, somehow, that the existence of the nation ought to be perpetuated for some purpose, for some mission to be fulfilled which is not yet defined, not yet clear. They feel that there is some brilliant star behind the clouded heavens which will soon break through the clouds and shower on them beams of light and waves of warmth to quicken them and lead them on the way to salvation — their own and that of all mankind. It is a vague feeling, a blurred vision (a stirring of dry bones), but it is there in the heart of every conscientious Jew. They feel that things cannot and ought not to go on as they were before; that something cataclysmic will happen, must happen, to save the Jewish people from extinction and lead them on to the destiny for which they have been elected and preserved. They feel that the only place where this greatest of all miracles will happen is in Israel — the Promised Land. Thus present-day Judaism, with hardly any significant exception, revolves around the State of Israel. Jews all over the world, whatever their religious or social views, feel that with the new State of Israel there lies their finest and the final hope of survival as a people. Therefore, weave your conversation with them around Israel. Knowing the Bible and the everlasting covenant you can readily confirm the Jew in his conviction, and clear up things for him in the light which to him is still nebulous but to you is already shining brightly. The future of the Jewish people according to prophecy really lies in the Promised Land. Thus the more you are informed about the Promised Land in prophecy and in its current events the more likely you are to touch and activate tender chords in the Jewish heart and get a harmonious response.

Yet, although Israel has now become, to most Jews, the center and circumference of "Judaism," large numbers of Jews feel impelled by some inner urge to cling to the old traditions. While the world around the Jew is cold, unfriendly, even hostile, he feels at home only among his own brethren, and the best bond of affinity is in the synagogue or the center — the religious home of the Jews throughout the diaspora — where he may always meet them.

Out of atavism, nostalgia, habit, inertia, or in honor of his parents' memory, and especially his spiritual longing to be an inseparable member of historic suffering Jewry, he will usually affiliate with an Orthodox synagogue. Some Jews, to compromise between their own liberal views and those of their observant parents, may join a conservative synagogue, which is halfway between Orthodoxy and Reform Judaism. Still others may think that they would derive enough "religion" and maintain a bond with fellow Jews, in the Reform Temple. Some who care little for religion are satisfied with Zionism alone — unaware of the fact that this, too, is a form of religion. Until recently there were quite a number of Jews who adhered to Socialism or Communism — this adherence, too, was a kind of religion. When Jews believe in some idea, they stick to it with religious fervor and are ready to sacrifice their all for its defense. Finally, there are also some Jews who are unconcerned and indifferent to Judaism in any form. All they want is to live as ordinary human beings without any national or religious commitments and problems, or social complexities. They want to be mixed and absorbed by the Gentile people around them.

ORTHODOXY

(Or "Traditional Judaism")

This as we have seen is by far the largest sect in Judaism. In principle though not always in practice, these Jews firmly believe that the Bible (Old Testament) is the revealed Word of God to His chosen people Israel, and that they ought to keep holy every iota of it, and live their whole life in accordance with it. Furthermore they still cling to the idea that since not everything in the Scriptures is clear to everyone the wise Rabbis are authorized to expound and elucidate difficult passages. And that whenever there arise new problems and the necessity for new laws and ordinances, the Rabbis have the authority to enact such laws, etc. But because nothing should be added nor subtracted from what has been written in the Torah, the Rabbis by some clever twist of a certain verse, word or even some dot, could sanction and incorporate their new precepts into the Torah as if it had been given by God to Moses on Sinai — even when some rabbinic laws circumvent or nullify the written Law of Moses.

In the course of the centuries, since the close of the Hebrew Canon of Scriptures, the Rabbis have introduced thousands of new laws that govern the whole life of the Jew, from cradle to grave, "from womb to tomb," in all his waking hours. From the moment of awakening until he falls asleep, he is to observe his religion as it is written: "Hear, O Israel: The Lord our God is one Lord. And thou shalt love the Lord thy God with all thine heart, and with all thy soul, and with all thy might. And these words, which I command thee this day, shall be in thine heart: And thou shalt teach them diligently unto thy children, and shalt talk of them when thou sittest in thine house, and when thou walkest by the way, and when thou liest down, and when thou risest up. And thou shalt bind them for a sign upon thine hand, and they shall be as frontlets between thine eyes. And thou shalt write them upon the posts of thy house, and on thy gates" (Deuteronomy 6:4-9). These six verses he repeats several times daily, and on various special occasions. This is his most solemn prayer; it is the essence of Judaism. It has been the very life of the observant Jew.

His frequent ablutions, his dressing, his eating, his walk and talk has been bound up with specified regulations and ceremonies. Besides his three daily prayers which are quite lengthy, there are "a hundred specified blessings" which he has to recite during each day. And there are the various feasts and fasts and memorial days which the Jew has to observe; and these holidays are extremely solemn and highly impressive. In short, all his life, day by day, is inseparable from his religion. Thus, as we have previously pointed out, to give up his religion has often been tantamount with giving up life itself.

Throughout the centuries the Jewish people submitted faithfully to the "Law" as the Rabbis taught it. Judaism has, rightly, often been called "Rabbinism." There were some exceptions. During the Second Temple there were the Sadducees who had their own interpretation of the Bible. Later (in Dispersion) there arose the Karaite sect, who denied the Rabbis' authority to do as they pleased with the Word of God.[2] The great mass of Jewry kept

---

[2] The Karaites in course of time seceded from traditional Rabbinic Judaism and kept strictly to the laws of the Bible *only*. Today there are only a few left of this sect.

strictly to Judaism which was, theoretically, composed of two parts, the *Written Law* which Moses wrote down at Sinai, and the *Oral Law* which Moses supposedly delivered to the Elders and by whom it was in later years entrusted to the Rabbis. It was only hundreds of years later when the Jews were dispersed and there was danger that the Oral part might be forgotten, that the Rabbis put these laws into writing. This Code came to be known as the "Talmud." This is the "Judaism" that has been recognized and established by Jewry (as a whole) through the ages. And this type of "Judaism" is what Orthodoxy wants to perpetuate (and no effort or cost is spared to keep it alive).

I want to stress here that a great many Jews are Orthodox only in name and affiliation, though there are large numbers who earnestly *try* to conform to the tenets and precepts of Orthodoxy. I say "try," because many of the Rabbinic laws are very difficult, some even impossible, to observe and obey in modern life. Especially the young generation could not and would not be subjugated to Orthodoxy as they see no sense in observing meaningless, obsolete practices.

DOCTRINES OF ORTHODOXY

According to traditional Judaism the Jew is to believe in the thirteen Articles of Faith formulated by Maimonides (1135-1204).

Although part of these are so defined as to distinguish between the Jewish and the Christian doctrines of faith, they are basically the same as those of Christianity. For instance, they believe in the unity of God, but this unity is so defined as to preclude any thought of plurality. Of course, as we shall later see, this has no biblical basis, since the very word which in the Hebrew Bible means "God" (Elohim) is in the plural. Among these doctrines are the "Coming of the Messiah," the "Resurrection of the dead," and divine retribution for man's acts.

The only real difference between the two faiths is that Judaism rejects the Messiahship of Jesus, as we shall see later when we discuss the Jewish contentions against Christ.

PRACTICES OF ORTHODOXY

1. *Kosher Food — (Dietary Laws)*

While many of the old practices have fallen into disuse in recent years, the greatest part of Jewry, especially the "Orthodox" Jews, still observe the so-called *Kosher* laws.

The observant Jew's life is, as we have seen, rigidly regulated by innumerable laws and customs. He is particularly punctilious and scrupulous in regard to his food. It sometimes seems that contemporary Orthodox Judaism is but a matter of prescribed eating and drinking known as *kosher*. Few domestic animals: wild beasts, birds and fish are Kosher — i.e., ritually fit to eat. The pig is especially taboo and abhorrent. The animals which are Kosher have to be slaughtered in a particular manner by an authorized pious man, and even then their meat has to be prepared ritualistically in order to render it fit to eat. And even then not all the Kosher foodstuffs may be mixed together. Milk products and meat products could not be eaten at the same meal. Separate vessels and utensils have to be kept for each of these two sorts of food.[3] The intake of food must be preceded and followed by a benediction. Each kind of food has a special benediction and the benediction after meals is quite lengthy.

Meals must also be preceded by ritual washing of the hands.

For the Sabbath and feast-days special food is prepared, and the meals are eaten "religiously," accompanied by singing of pious sacred songs.

2. *Prayer*

The observant Jew's life was taken up mostly by prayer, or rather the reciting of prescribed "prayers." As soon as he awakes from the night's sleep he is obliged to recite a certain prayer, then after proper ablution he is to go to the synagogue for the morning service which on week days, lasts about an hour, and on Sabbath, festival, and fast days, several hours. In the late afternoon and in the evening there are again two services (usually combined) at the synagogue which every Jew should attend. (See Chapter on "Prayer Life").

3. *Sabbath and Feast Days*[4]

The Sabbath, and to a large extent also the festivals, is to the observant Jew a *holy* day in the fullest sense of the word. It is a day fully dedicated to the LAW. From Friday evening to Saturday night the Jew is aware that he must keep it holy. No physical work or carrying of any burden is done, no business is transacted, no secular, profane thoughts are harbored in his mind. Most of the day is spent in prayer and in the study of sacred books.

[3] See KASHER in chapter on "Customs."
[4] See Chapter 7.

The prescribed meals, too, are a kind of divine service, and even sleep is counted as a virtue — because the Sabbath and festivals are to be observed joyfully and pleasantly.

These (Kosher, Prayer and Holy Days) are the three pillars that uphold the structure called "Orthodoxy," but as mentioned before there are thousands of other laws and usages, which contemporary Orthodox Jews try to keep somehow or find some excuse for evading or overlooking them.

Thus, if there is still a sect that exercises some zeal for God, though "without knowledge" as Paul termed it, it is the Orthodox sect. For the other sects have not much zeal, and less knowledge.

This is also the only sect that holds the Bible (Old Testament) as the supreme authority on "Judaism," because, they firmly believe, it is the peremptory Word of God.

Reform Judaism

Those who do not adhere to tradition but yet would not abandon or repudiate Judaism altogether call themselves *Reformed*.

This religious movement is about one hundred years old. It is the outgrowth of the age of *enlightenment*.

In Western European countries, as previously mentioned, where the Jews were allowed to come out of their ghettos and live with the other citizens and enjoy the same civil rights and privileges, many of the Jews thought the time ripe to shake off old shackles and join the new tide of equality and liberty. Here was a chance "to be like all the people." See Ezekiel 20:32. To achieve this end, the Jewish religion which tended to keep the Jews apart from Gentiles, had to be modified. But how may man modify and change the God-given Word? Well, there were liberal Rabbis who began teaching that the Word was not God-given. Thus neither the Bible nor the Talmud had any authority which the Jew must obey. This new movement underwent many radical changes. Some of its leaders held that all usages which tended to keep the Jews apart from their Gentile neighbors should be abrogated: such were circumcision, the dietary laws, the keeping of Sabbath on Saturday, praying in a foreign language (in Hebrew), praying for the coming of the Messiah and return to Zion, which suggest that the Jews are foreigners, and wishing to return to their ancient home. These and many other such laws and customs were abolished and later re-established partly or entirely according to time and place.

Zionism, which was formerly taboo to Reform Judaism, is now sponsored by many of its leaders. Prayers are conducted partly in Hebrew and partly in the language of the country of residence. Some laws, as the dietary Kosher laws, are left to the conscience of the individual.

This "sect" is by far smaller, but more conspicuous, than the Orthodox. Their "temples" (synagogues) are more imposing and impressive; their Rabbis are masters of rhetoric and oratory; they are good "mixers" in society and know how to encourage the friendship of Gentiles to Jews and Judaism. The services are held in the manner of the Christians, accompanied by organ music, men and women are seated together and the men are bare headed.

The members of the Temple are generally of the upper class, merchants and professional people. Except on the High Holidays they seldom attend the services of the Temple, because they have little time to spend for it, and less faith in it. They claim to be very proud of their "Judaism," because of its high ethical and social values.

Reform Judaism does not believe in the coming of a "Messiah" or in anything supernatural, but many of its leaders and spokesmen have expressed their high regard for Jesus — as a great teacher and reformer.

CONSERVATISM

This sect is "Made in America." It occupies a position midway between Orthodoxy and Reform Judaism. The latter, it seems to them, has diverged and strayed too far away from traditional Judaism, while Orthodoxy is too antiquated and outgrown for modern times. They opine that Judaism, if it is to remain alive, must "grow" and undergo the natural changes of growth. In other words it has to comply with and conform to contemporary life and changing conditions. Generally it is much nearer to Orthodoxy than to Reform Judaism. It retains many of the traditional laws and usages, but the individual may modify and adjust his religion to his needs. To a great extent this adjustment and modification of old laws to modern life is in general the practice of most contemporary Jews of all sects.

CONSTRUCTIONISM
("Made in America")

This is quite a recent innovation in American Judaism and has not many followers. They hold that Judaism is a civilization rather than a religion. It is a particular kind of life of a particular people who have their own language, literature, law, and customs which may be called "religion." All these things may be changed to fit time and place. For example, the Jews of America may speak the American language, read its literature and observe its laws and customs.

In short, Judaism was intended for the Jew, and not the Jew for Judaism. This recalls what Jesus said about the Sabbath, but there is a vast difference. It denies the existence of a personal God and thus also divine revelation, consequently there is no "chosen people," etc.

Although they have their rabbis and their synagogues and services, yet their queer sort of "religion" is so far away from what is generally understood by the term religion, that we may dismiss it from further consideration as an unimportant segment of Judaism.

ZIONISM

Zionism does not claim to be a religious sect, and many agnostics and atheists are among its adherents. Yet if we consider the basic principles of Zionism we may conclude that this is the real Judaism — the true religion of Israel. Otherwise, why should it (Zionism) want to go "*back*" to Zion; and by what right may it put a claim to that far away strip of land which, according to secular common opinion, belongs to someone else?

The "non-religious" Zionist may find two or three reasons why Palestine belongs to the Jewish people and why the Jews should go back thereto. But, if pressed with questions, he will finally resort to the Bible as the legal charter saying that God, the Lord of all lands, gave this particular land to the Jews. When you ask him why they should want to "go back" after an absence of 1,900 years, what assurance they have that it would be better for them over there politically, economically, physically or spiritually, he will, after evasive replies, have only one answer: The Jews feel an inner urge that they have to go "back," that they feel something grand and glorious is going to happen there, that they have a most sacred mission to fulfill. Zionists, consciously or subconsciously, are a religious sect in the truest meaning of religion, although they may not observe certain rites.

INDIFFERENT JEWS

There is a large number of Jews who do not identify themselves with any particular Jewish Segment. Some indifferently belong to the one or the other segment, on social or economical grounds. For these or similar reasons, a Jew may belong to two or even more opposing segments. He is not obliged to do much in order to be "a member" as long as he dutifully pays the required membership fees. There are also a great many who do not "belong" at all. They find that they can get along nicely without having to be "affiliated." Then there are the socialists and communists who think that religion would not help the Jews, nor any religion help any people. They claim that the only salvation for both, Jew and non-Jew, is socialism or communism, which would equalize human society in dividing the wealth of the world according to the needs of each individual without any distinction between race, sex, etc.

Up to a few years ago socialism (in its various forms) had a firm grip on Jewish workers and intellectuals. Now, after Communist Russia has demonstrated how socialism works when being materialized, its Jewish adherents have become totally disillusioned. Only a few fanatics and paid propagandists still cling to it.

Most of the Indifferent Jews have little knowledge of the Bible, yet could, with the Lord's help, be led to it and its wonderful revelations.

Summary of Segments

Summing up the segments, those that we have mentioned and others that we did not think it necessary to mention, we may roughly divide Jewry into three general parts (from a religious viewpoint).

1. Those who believe the Bible as the Word of God.
2. Those who do not believe so, who waver or doubt whether all or only part of the Bible is His Word.
3. The indifferent — those who do not care whether it is right or wrong, true or false. They think that one can get along without religion.

As already mentioned contemporary Judaism has practically no religious divisions which take their sectarian affiliation very seriously. With few exceptions modern Jews, unlike their forefathers, are not eager to endure persecution, inconveniences, torture or death in defense of their religious convictions.

However, Judaism (in its various segments) is now undergoing a radical transformation which will bring forth a new type of Jew — the type whom the prophets longed to see — the type which the Lord promised Abraham, when He said that in his seed all the nations will be blessed. Summing it up; the Jews who lived traditionally "Jewish" are rare exhibitions from the past. I still remember them. I was born and reared in their midst. But one

should have some knowledge of them because one could not understand the present-day Jews without knowing whence they came.
The Jews of today are the products, offspring and heirs of those
of yesterday. The Judaism of their fathers has become inadequate,
impossible for present day life, but they still claim Judaism as their
priceless heritage, their dearest possession, transmitted to them
from hoary antiquity (which has no practical use).

Only, they are at a loss what to do with this dearest possession,
this glorious heirloom.

Some Christians view this present indifference of the Jews
toward Judaism as a calamity. But it is not so. They may be
likened unto a receptacle which was filled with water and became
stagnant and contaminated. The water has to be poured out and
the receptacle sterilized before filling it again with pure water.

There is a stirring of the dry bones and great events which
will yet occur until God will revive them with His spirit and they
will again be His Holy People ready to fulfill the mission entrusted to them since the Covenant with their patriarch Abraham.

Really it is not essential for us to know with what sect or
party the Jew is affiliated. All we need know is what is his conception of God and what he thinks of the Bible. And this we may
discover easily after our initial talk with him, soon after we have
gained his attention and confidence.

There are two topics which are bound, unfailingly, to arouse
the attention of every Jew today: 1. The State of Israel; 2. Anti-
Semitism. Just start on any of these subjects and you will get his
immediate attention.

Furthermore, since these two topics are the heart of evangelization (Anti-Semitism — the result of the fall from grace, and the
State of Israel — the beginning of the return to grace) you may
enlarge upon them and continue your conversation around these
two; or rather condense the two into one topic: *The Solution of
the Jewish Problem,*" or if you find him truly religious, call it:
"The Jews' Reconciliation With God."

CHAPTER IV

THE JEWISH RELIGION

Just as you cannot find a suitable and generally accepted definition of "Jew," so you cannot find any such definition for "Jewish Religion." And yet everyone knows that there are such people as "Jews." In fact, they are, in a sense, "ubiquitous," and everyone knows that there exists a "Jewish Religion."

Ask the average Jew what is his religion and he will unhesitatingly. reply that it is the belief in the "Torah." If you further ask: "What is the 'Torah'?" — then the answer will be hesitatingly vague, depending on the religious segment to which he belongs. Generally the "Torah" is defined as the "Bible," meaning the Old Testament, in particular the five books of Moses. But usually all the laws that the Rabbis have ever enacted are included in the word "Torah."

Now there is not a single word in the whole Bible which could be translated as "religion," in the sense in which this term is generally used. There is nothing in the Bible which might be defined as "Jewish Religion." The word *dath* which in modern Hebrew means "religion" is mentioned only in post-exilic books of the Bible (in Daniel, Ezra and Esther), and there it means, "law," "custom," "command," "sentence." Another word which in modern Hebrew is often used as "religion," *emunah,* is to be found in the Bible, but there it means, "trust," "belief," "faith," "steadiness"; there is nothing in it that suggests worship, devotion, etc., which we usually associate with religion.

Nowhere in the Bible (Old Testament) does it say what a Jew should believe in, although it tells him what to *do* and what *not to do.*[1] Neither is there anything in the post-biblical Talmudic books which might be taken as a "Creed." The Jew was enjoined to *obey the Law of God.*

[1] Recently a well-known rabbi let it be known that a Jew does not even have to believe in the existence of God in order to be called a "Jew."

The Jewish people were not *commanded* to *believe* in the existence of God nor that He revealed Himself on Sinai and gave them the Law (Torah), although this belief was a matter of course and self evident. But they were *taught to believe,* and they generally, firmly, believed that *God and the Torah and Israel are bound together as one,* and when they really served God it was with all their heart and all their mind. They were always aware that God is particularly their own God and that they are particularly His own people. This conviction came after long years of preaching by the prophets and after much and repeated castigation which followed their wandering astray — away from God during the "first commonwealth" (when they often relapsed into idol worship). The destruction of the first Temple brought about a radical change of heart. Then the belief in God was firmly, lastingly and immutably inculcated in every Jewish heart.

During the "Second Temple," and up to the time of Christ, the Jewish people (with the exception of the Sect of the Sadducees who, although politically influential, were yet a small minority) unwaveringly believed in God, and in the Bible as the holy and true Word of God. This belief included the "coming of the Messiah" and the "resurrection of the dead."

It is this *"belief,"* besides the various ritual practices, which might be called "the Jewish Religion." The need for writing down a creed, to be recited and reaffirmed daily was not felt till about the twelfth century when the Jews had to fortify and defend their religion against the onslaught of other religions; in some countries it was Mohammedanism, in others Christianity. Various Jewish authorities put forward various "credos," but only that formulated by Maimonides, the "Rambam," was generally accepted and later embodied into the daily "prayer." At the beginning of the morning service it is recited in verse and at the end of the service in prose. This creed, in Hebrew "Ani Ma'amin" — "I believe," consists of thirteen Articles of Faith (or properly "Principles of Faith," see page 181).

Maimonides writes that he devoted much time and thought on the formulation of these principles, yet one may wonder why this genius, this master of fine style, simplicity and logic had not made these principles as clear and simple as he did his other writings. They are *not* clear. They evoke many questions. They need elucidation and there is only confusion in them.

Because this "creed," which is generally accepted as the essence of the Jewish religion, is often used as an argument against

Christianity, it is fitting here to show some of its defects and discrepancies. For example, only one of his thirteen principles he bases on the Bible by quoting a fitting passage (see Tenth Principle). All others he takes for granted. On what biblical passage does he base his Sixth Principle, declaring that all that the Prophets said *is* true? And why is it necessary to have a special "credo" that the prophecy of Moses was *true?* Why is Six in the present tense, and Seven in the past tense? Who were the Prophets that preceded Moses (7)? In Principle Eight, what is meant by the "whole Torah"? Does it mean only the Pentateuch, or the whole Bible, or the Bible plus its interpretation of the Rabbis as recorded in the Talmud? On what passage of the Bible does he base the Principle Thirteen of the resurrection of the dead?

His Principles on the existence and nature of God are vaguely stated. It may be said that they were meant to be more as an abnegation of Christianity than as an assertion of Judaism.

We may divide his Principles into two sections: 1. Those that refer to the belief in the infinite, incomprehensible, inimaginable Being — God. 2. The belief in all that is written in the Torah — *because it was given by God.*

The Christian conception of God, according to Scriptures, is One infinite Being who, in order to create the world, to rule it and to communicate with man, has revealed Himself in finite form of man or by the Holy Spirit. Thus He is conceived as a triune Being, expressed in the doctrine of the "Trinity." The God of Maimonides is an infinite unit that precludes all revelation or materialization as becoming "flesh." While the Hebrew Bible in defining the unity of God uses the word "echad," which does not exclude a plurality in one, Maimonides uses the word "yachid" which designates an absolute unit, or singleness and solitariness. This change he introduced to show that the Christian conception of God as a trinity is foreign to Judaism.

Maimonides seems to have labored under two contradictory ideas about God. On the one hand he was a faithful follower (and adherent) of the Rabbis and he made it incumbent on the Jews to observe all the laws which the Rabbis (up to his time) had enacted. On the other hand he was a firmly convinced rationalist, steeped in Aristotelian philosophy, whose God could be defined or conceived only by negatives, i.e., He is not good, not bad, not big, not small, has no desires, does not care, and of course has no mouth to speak, no ears to hear, no hands to do anything, etc.

The Bible, however, tells of God revealing Himself to man, loving, hating, getting angry, repenting, speaking, walking; in short, becoming man, becoming flesh. The Rambam (Maimonides) explains elsewhere such anthropomorphisms as allegories and metaphors. In this he followed the Alexandrian school of interpretation of the Bible. According to such interpretation of the Bible God could not have come down to Sinai and there declared His Law. But if this were so, if it is allegory, or pure fancy, why does he want the Jews to believe that Moses (real flesh and blood) received the Torah on Sinai and that this Torah is *true* and therefore binding on every Jew? If the story of Abraham and his dealings with God as told in the Bible were pure allegory, as allegorists say, why should the Jews (even the so-called rational and Reform Jews) today have to circumcise their flesh in order to be a Jew? All on account of that "ancient fable" of Abraham and his fictitious covenant? On account of another ancient "allegory," as that of Jacob struggling with the angel, according to the Bible, Jews of today, as those of old, have to observe certain *Kosher* laws, which entail a great deal of trouble and cost. Maimonides, the great rationalist, the allegorist, insists that the Jews must obey, must keep meticulously all such laws! He wrote large volumes compiling all these laws; 613 laws of the Bible, and hundreds of others which the post-biblical rabbis built around them.

Maimonides "believed in the Bible," because, according to him, it is all compatible with human reasoning. What seems to be irrational is just a kind of fable having some inner meaning. According to him *"the literal sense must give way when it contradicts the postulates of philosophy,"* and yet according to him all legal enactments must be taken and observed literally. *His allegorism is thus confined between the barriers of his rationalism on the one hand and his fidelity to tradition on the other.*

Such inconsistency may be found in many of the arguments of the rabbis, particularly of the liberal type. In contra-distinction to Christianity they like to boast that Judaism is a rational religion. They like to quote Maimonides, who is considered to be one of the greatest authorities on Judaism, who allows reasoning powers full play in investigating biblical precepts, to justify scriptural religion to the human intellect, to verify the fundamental concepts of religion on purely rational grounds. How much rationalism underlies the thousands of laws (e.g. the Kosher Laws) which comprise the religion called "Judaism"?

According to the rationalists, God, the Jewish God, is so perfect that He could not have walked the earth in the guise of a man, as the Christians believe, lived a man's life and died a death of suffering. "To say that God put on the garb of flesh is pure idolatry" — so the rationalist rabbis say in contention with Christianity. Here again is inconsistency: Why should God, the infinite, the perfect, not be able to put on the garb of flesh? Is He not omnipotent? Could He do everything else, but not put on the garb of flesh, and walk the earth?

Suppose God did not reveal Himself to man in the "garb of flesh" or in any other irrational manner, suppose He did not appear to Adam, Noah, the Patriarchs, to Moses, to the prophets, etc., as the Bible tells us. Suppose He did not choose the Jews as His people (how could the "Infinite" do such a thing!) and did not command them, do this, and don't do that. Suppose He did not promise rewards for pleasing Him, and punishment for displeasing Him — suppose all these stories of the Bible are fiction and fancy of an ancient, primitive, immature people. Strike out all this "nonsense" of the Jewish Bible, what will there be left? What would there be left to justify a "Judaism," whatever it be?

The great Maimonides whose "God" is some inconceivable idea, some "Not," should not have linked this "credo" with that of giving the Torah on Sinai since the two are contradictory. Indeed, his impersonal, unfathomable, philosophical God has almost nothing to do with Judaism; for Judaism has come into being with the revealed God, with the personal God, with the One who *has* taken on the "garb of flesh." The first sentence of the Constitution, the preamble, of Judaism which was given on Sinai, begins with "I am Jehovah *thy Gods*[2] who has brought *thee* out of Egypt. . . ." Not "I am the infinite, the inconceivable . . ." When God revealed Himself to Moses, in the Burning Bush, He did not introduce Himself as God of the universe, but as the *Gods* of his father, "the Gods of Abraham . . ."; and when He sent him to His people, He instructed him to tell them that Jehovah the *Gods* of their fathers, the Gods of Abraham . . . had sent him. All through the Bible He is the Gods of the fathers, the particularly Jewish Gods, the personal one. Very seldom is He mentioned as God of

[2] In this quotation I understood the word "Gods" because in the original — in the Hebrew Bible — it says "Gods" — implying God as a plurality.

the universe. So also in the Jewish prayers it is "our *Gods* and the Gods of our fathers. . . ."

God is revealed. God makes Himself understood to man in the way man is capable of understanding. Of course the Old Testament prophets as well as the New Testament disciples of Christ knew that God is infinite, indescribable, but they like to think of Him, pray to Him as the father in whose *image* He created His children. A father speaks to his little children in the language of little children, otherwise they would not understand him.

After much opposition the Jewish people adopted the Creed of the thirteen articles of faith but the average Jew does not understand the "credo" in the single God of Maimonides anymore than he would understand the triune God as is the credo of Christianity. Nor does the average Jew speculate about the nature of God, whether He is immanent or transcendent. He believes that God is omnipresent, but that God, as taught by Maimonides, so far transcends human comprehension that all positive descriptions of Him are inappropriate, foreign to the Jewish mind. To him, to the average Jew, God sits in heaven (sometimes they call it "Gan Eden" — the Garden of Eden) on His throne of Glory, surrounded by the angels (Cherubim and Seraphim) and by the saints who after death have been going up to be with Him. He, or the "Shekinah" (very few Jews have a clear conception of what that means) who used to be in the Tabernacle, or later in the two Temples often comes down to the Synagogue or wherever Jews pray as a congregation.

The Jews believe in the same God as does the average Christian ascribing to Him the same attributes. The only difference is that while the Christian can by the doctrine of the Trinity reconcile the conception of the infinite God with the conception of the personal God who has revealed Himself to man, either by taking on the "garb of man" or by inspiration, the Jew is not quite sure of that. He often explains that, by saying that it is the angels who act in His stead and take on human form. The wise and well-informed Christian may easily prove to him that the "Trinity" is not only a better solution to that problem — of God revealing Himself to man — but the only true one.

MANY BOOKS

Many scholarly books have been written on Judaism, or on The Jewish Religion, most of them in America, but hardly any of these books are written objectively. It seems that the only aim of most of these books is to prove that Judaism is much better than Christianity. One may wonder for whom such books were intended. The observant Jew does not want any proofs. The non-observant Jew does not care for any proof since religion, especially rites and rituals, does not interest him. The same may be said about the Christian. The nominal Christian who cares little about religion is not likely to read such books, while the true Christian would likely not be influenced by them, since to him, high moral standards, noble thoughts, etc., as Judaism is pictured in those books, is not enough to bring sinful man to God — to him there is no way to God but through His Son. Whatever is the purpose of those books, they generally present to the reader only a blurred picture of Judaism. They conceal a great deal, they misinterpret a great deal, they exaggerate a great deal and even mis-state a great deal. In short, they often tell you half-truths, and even less, and make you believe that they are full truths. Their "Judaism" is *not* Judaism. However, most of them agree, and we agree with them, that "Judaism" is more a "way of life" than it is a religion. It *is not* a mere recitation of a certain creed, visiting a house of worship at specified times, having prayer once in a while.

The average Jew's conception of Judaism is as it was *in practice* all through the dispersion: It was a total subordination, a complete dedication of all thoughts and actions to the will of God (as interpreted and enacted by the rabbis). If the present day Jew does no longer practice this old rabbinic Judaism it is not that he has come to a new conception of Judaism, but because it has become too confused to him, too difficult. In their perplexity most contemporary Jews (of all segments) came to think that by modifying and adjusting the old laws and customs to modern life they can keep Judaism alive (a crippled, moribund Judaism, some semblance of it). Let us have a glance at the old now vanishing Judaism as the observant Jew had practiced it and a great many Orthodox Jews still tenaciously adhere to it.[3]

The Jew who observes Judaism[4] awakes in the morning with the sure consciousness of the divine presence. This consciousness is with him all through his waking hours, till he falls asleep at night. Accordingly all his time is filled with worship. On each

[3] See chapter on "Segments."

[4] Again I want to emphasize that observant Jews have, during the last few decades, been rapidly disappearing.

week-day he spends at the synagogue about three hours in prayer, on the Sabbath and holy days more hours are given to prayer (See Chapter on Prayer). All through the day there are various occasions for benedictions. A great many Jews dedicate most of the time to the study of the Torah. Even artisans and businessmen find spare time for such study. Not only the Jew's prayers and study, but also his eating, drinking, dressing, washing, etc., all is dedicated to God's glory; everything is done according to prescription, everything intertwined with ritual and benediction. Fringes, Phylacteries, and Mezuzoth are to remind the Jew of his duties to God, as it is written in Deuteronomy 6:4-9 (at home, on the way, on lying down, and rising up). (See also Deuteronomy 11:13-21, and Numbers 15:37-41). Thus Judaism is a way of life — a constant uninterrupted living with God, from the cradle till the grave, or as one said it: "from the womb to the tomb."

Imagine what such zeal — zeal for godly things — would do to mankind if the zeal were coupled with true knowledge, as Paul expressed it in Romans 10:1-3. The Lord who has chosen this people, and trained them to such religiosity, to such zeal, is about to fill them with knowledge, as the waters cover the sea (see Isaiah 11:9). According to Jeremiah 31:33 — "This shall be the covenant that I will make with the house of Israel; After those days, saith the Lord, I will put my law in their inward parts, and write it in their hearts; and will be their God, and they shall be my people."

REWARD

Two principles[5] have nourished the zeal and the power of endurance of the Jew to keep and practice the Torah tenaciously and meticulously in the face of almost insurmountable difficulties and at great sacrifice — often with supreme sacrifice. These were the hopes of *the coming of the Messiah* and the *Resurrection*. With the coming of the Messiah the Jewish people as a nation will be rewarded for their faithfulness to God, and with the Resurrection, every individual will be rewarded according to his deeds. The more a man suffers in this world for God's sake, the greater will be his reward in the world to come.

We shall have a special chapter on the Jewish belief in the coming of the Messiah. But we shall have here a few words on the "World to Come."

The last of the thirteen *Articles of Faith* expresses the belief

[5] The 12th and 13th Principles of the Thirteen, formulated by Maimonides.

in the resurrection of the dead. But it does not state when, where, how and to what purpose will the dead arise, nor whether these will be Jews only or also Gentiles. So also is the preceding Eleventh Article very vague when it says that God rewards those that keep His commandments, and punishes those that transgress them. It does not say when and how this retribution takes place. It does not even say, or hint, that a man may avert punishment, by repentance or atonement.

The Jews faithfully repeat daily this thirteen-fold confession of faith because the rabbis told them to do so — although they are quite confused as to their exact meaning. Yet they derive consolation in the promise of a glorious future — or reward.

What the Jew generally believes, is that in this world the righteous may suffer, and the wicked may prosper, but the real retribution is in the "World to Come." In Hebrew it is "Olam haBa," and to this world comes each and every individual right after his death. The body may disintegrate and crumble and wait till after the coming of the Messiah, when it will come to life again, but the soul soon after death comes before the Heavenly Tribunal where it is judged according to its merits and demerits in this world.

Every Jew is entitled to a share in the "World to Come" but it usually takes a year of expiation by torment in hell (some kind of purgatory) till the soul is totally purged, purified from the sins it committed in this world. In order to alleviate the pangs and pains of hell the survivor's next of kin (only male) recites the "Kaddish" at the three daily prayers during the year after death. To make it still easier for the dead he learns daily a portion of the "Mishnah" or hires someone to learn it in his stead. On certain holidays there is also a special *Memorial Service* for the souls in which the sons (and daughters — in the female section of the synagogue) participate.

The soul — according to common belief — does not sever all its connections with this world. For the first seven days, after its departure from the body, it is a great deal "at home" with its loved ones. Then for another three weeks, altogether thirty days it frequents less its earthly abode, and gradually it is weaned away from this world. But there always remains some connection between the living and the dead. Jews have often gone to the graves of relatives invoking the help of the departed souls; they are asked to intercede for the living who were in need of speedy succor. The graves (sepulchers) of saints are frequented, especially on their anniversaries (memorial days), and are invoked for intercession before the "Throne of Glory."

Formerly Jews generally believed in transmigration of souls ("gilgul"). For some reason the departed soul may have to be born again in this world, to have another chance and amend wrong done before. It may even transmigrate into an animal for a certain period and for a certain purpose. Sometimes some wicked soul, instead of submitting to Judgment, enters and possesses some living person resulting in his or her mental illness and premature death (see Dibbuk).[6] Some of the Chassidic rabbis were known as proficient experts at expelling such evil spirits from the bodies of the possessed.

These beliefs have undergone great changes. The "dibbuk" and the "gilgul" are now considered more as folklore and bygone superstition, but the Jews as a whole still have an ingrained ineradicable belief in life after death and that the departed "near and dear" are still *near* and dear. The Jews including many of the "moderns," "reformed" and skeptics are still very careful in the observance of *"Yarzeit," Kaddish* and *memorial service* and *Hazkarath Neshamoth.*[7] To them it is not a mere honoring the memory of the dead, but a renewal of communion with them, and a refastening the ties that bind the living with the beloved dead ones.

Is this "cult of the dead," as one may call it, an integral part of Judaism? Although many "exponents" of Judaism say "no," my answer is "yes." Because as we have seen, "Judaism" is the peculiar way Jews live, think and practice. This cult has been lived and practiced by Jews for ages.

I found it necessary to enlarge upon this part of Judaism because the so-called exponents of Judaism, in contrasting it with Christianity, claim that it is pure logic and common sense, even compatible with "science," etc., that there is no mediation, intercession in Judaism, that there is no original sin, that every man is judged on his own merits and that men are generally good, and God is good and all-merciful, and therefore always forgiving human frailties and thus not likely to punish cruelly any transgressions of His Law. These exponents sometimes rudely scoff, ridicule, sometimes politely hint at the stories and miracles of the New Testament and show how irrational they are, how foreign to Judaism which is all rational, all reasonable.

[6] See "Vocabulary."
[7] See "Vocabulary."

These "scholarly" exponents of Judaism, especially in America and Britain, are of the "reform" liberal type to whom traditional Judaism is as foreign and obnoxious to taste and thought as it is to Christians. But preferring to remain Jews they reform, or deform, Judaism, fitting it to their own tastes and thought by culling passages from the Bible and rabbinic books — out of their context. They are clever writers and speakers, but they stand alone. Their sort of Judaism is but a creation of their own image, whereas the Jewish people as a whole have, through the ages, believed and observed a Judaism which is radically different from that of the modern "exponents" whose books, seemingly, are intended only for "export" — for Christians.

Contrary to the liberals, who teach that the Jews have been exiled from their ancient homeland, *not* for their sins, but only for the benefit of the world — to teach the Goyim (Gentiles) the true faith, the Jewish people know and continually confirm it in their prayers, that it is for their sins that they were exiled and are continually praying for forgiveness and for bringing them *back* to their ancient promised land.

In opposition to the expositions of the liberals, the Jews have believed in original sin, have believed that they could never be justified before God, and only for the sake of the Covenants He made with their forefathers, and for His own sake could they dare ask for His grace and pardon. They have believed that God is compassionate, but they also know that He is vengeful, when necessary. They often felt His hand, and contrary to the modern spokesmen of Judaism, the Jews have believed in just retribution, in the "world to come," in an abode of bliss (Gan Eden) and another of woe (Gehenom). They have always believed in the power of intercession and mediation, and in vicarious atonement. Not only does the Jewish Bible testify to these common beliefs, but the Jewish literature through the ages does so (except the few English writing "exponents" of the latter days).

In short, although there is a wall of partition between traditional Judaism and Christianity, it is not so formidable as not to be demolished. Both are really one and the same religion — the religion of the Bible. It may seem as a daring statement but it is true: original Christianity is original Judaism. It is the rabbinic exposition on the one hand and Gentile influence on the other hand that has accentuated the parting of the ways. This "wall of partition" has to be demolished, has to be removed, for the peace and salvation of mankind. According to prophecy the Jewish people will do this job after they have learned that this is *their* job.

CHAPTER V

THE PRAYER LIFE OF THE OBSERVANT JEW[1]

The whole life of the observant Jew is wrapped in prayer. He awakes in the morning and goes to sleep at night with a prayer on his lips. During the day he goes to the synagogue for three long prayers (in the morning, afternoon and evening). Besides the three services at the synagogue there are the prayers which are recited at home. A good Jew has to recite at least one hundred benedictions during the day. He must not eat or drink anything without certain specified blessings before and after it, and there are special benedictions for each kind of food; and not only for food, but for each time he experiences an extraordinary sight, sound or smell. In Yiddish the prescribed recitation of the three prayers is called "davnen."

His conversation, too, is interspersed frequently with some pious words as, "Praise be to God," "Thank God," "If God wills," "With the help of God," "May God avert it" (some evil), "May God protect us," etc. As in conversation, so also in correspondence; the Jew is ever mindful of God, so every letter begins with: "Blessed be God" or "With the help of God," etc.

Even when some misfortune befalls him, he is to praise God. Upon hearing of the death of someone dear to him, he is to say, "Blessed be the truthful judge." There is the pious adage, "Whatever the All Compassionate does, He does it for the best."[2]

And there is the "Thillim" — the Psalms — a steady companion of the pious Jew. Not only are Psalms to be recited on various occasions, in times of trouble, anxiety, etc., but he likes to fill in every idle moment at home, at the synagogue, at his work, on his travels

---

[1] Again we must caution the reader that the historic — the traditional — type of Judaism (including prayer life) is rapidly vanishing. However, we think that every Christian should be acquainted with it as the background of contemporary Jewry.

[2] The Jew is careful not to take the name of God in vain, so that when not in prescribed and fixed prayer, he generally uses instead, the word *haShem* — "the name" — thus *Baruch haShem* translated is "blessed be the name."

— with Psalms either by reading or from memory. Some Jews know all 150 Psalms by heart, although with many Jews it is more "prayer reciting" than actually praying.

HISTORY OF PRAYER

Let us take a glance at the history of the Jewish prayer. The word "Tefillah," the Hebrew word for "prayer," is derived from the root "palal" which means "to think," "to hope," "to judge" and also "to fall down," "to bow." It is "to fall" that probably served as root for prayer since prayer was originally generally performed by prostration or bowing down before God.[3]

With the Jews, prayer is as old as the beginning of their race. Indeed, according to Jewish tradition and legend, the three daily prayers were first instituted by the three patriarchs. Moses prayed, so did Joshua and the other prophets and men of God. King David is better known as the author of the Psalms, as the "sweet singer of Israel," than for his epoch-making deeds (mostly by his wars). His Psalms are, and will ever be, the best prayer book in the world. We find Solomon in prayer at the dedication of the Temple which he dedicated as a "House of Prayer" for all peoples. (See I Kings 8). Isaiah (56:7) also refers to this Sanctuary as the "House of prayer" to all the nations: "Even them will I bring to my holy mountain, and make them joyful in my house of prayer: their burnt-offerings and their sacrifices shall be accepted upon mine altar; for mine house shall be called an house of prayer for all people."

Prayer during the First Temple was more of a personal nature, where each worshiper expressed voluntarily and spontaneously his feelings and devotion to God, petitioning Him for help or thanking Him for help He had already rendered him. But it seems that there was also some kind of communal prayer, besides the daily sacrificial rites, which were (especially during the Second Temple) accompanied by orchestras of various musical instruments.

The necessity for communal prayer probably began to be felt after the reforms were instituted by King Josiah when sacrificial rites were limited only to the Temple in Jerusalem. The Jews who

[3] The various meanings of *Pallal* have led to the (mis)translation into English of I Samuel 2:25, "If one man sin against another, the judge shall judge him; but if a man sin against the Lord, who shall intreat for him? Notwithstanding they hearkened not unto the voice of their father, because the Lord would slay them." While the Hebrew words for "judge" and "intreat" (other versions have different translations) are about the same, both might better be translated by "intercede" or "mediate."

lived far away from Jerusalem felt that they ought to have a "House of Prayer" in their vicinity ("a lesser Temple"), where they could study the Torah and pray.

After the destruction of the First Temple and the cessation of the sacrificial rites, the Jews felt all the more the need for prayer to replace the sacrifices, as Hosea preached (14:2) " — so will we render the calves of our lips." Thus arose that typically Jewish institution (nothing like it in all the world) which we call "synagogue" or in Hebrew "Beth — Knesseth," a house of Congregation, for prayer and for study and often also for various meetings of communal importance. (See chapter on The Jewish Community — the Synagogue.)

During the Second Temple, although the daily sacrifices were reinstated, prayer both private and communal continued not only in the synagogue of the Dispersion but also in Judea and even in Jerusalem and in the Temple. Communal prayer in the synagogue has come to be considered not only as a supplement of the sacrifices of the Temple but as a divine service in itself.

Jesus, who Himself often prayed to the Father and urged His followers to pray, preferred secret prayer to that which was practiced ceremoniously and ostentatiously in the synagogue. Yet His objections were only against public prayers as practiced by hypocrites and by the heathen. See Matthew 6.

After the destruction of the Second Temple, prayer at the synagogue had replaced the Temple worship entirely. Thus, wherever there arose a Jewish settlement, however small, they built themselves a synagogue. From the New Testament we learn that wherever Paul went in his journeyings, he nearly always found a synagogue where he could start his preaching of the Gospel. "For Moses of old time hath in every city them that preach him, being read in the synagogues every sabbath day" (Acts 15:21). (See chapter on The Jewish Community — the Synagogue.)

It is difficult to state at what point public communal prayer became obligatory; nor do we know exactly of what those common prayers consisted. They were no doubt a slow development which included some of the Psalms and other portions of the Bible and later also of the Talmud as well as Jewish poetry. Some early rabbis were against fixed prayers at fixed times. Even after the Second Temple when the daily prayers were fixed and obligatory, some rabbis taught that God would better be served by the study of His Law, rather than by prayer. Some of the ancient rabbis prayed but seldom.

By the time of Jesus there were already certain prescribed prayers to be recited daily. There was the prayer known by the term "Sh'mone Esrei" — "Eighteen" — because it was composed of eighteen benedictions. There was also the "Sh'ma"[4] and probably some others (which some congregation or individual chose to include, especially certain Psalms).

After the Second Temple, when prayer was the only kind of worship that could substitute the sacrifices, there were many additions not only in petition and supplication, mainly for the common welfare, especially for the restoration of the Temple, but also of adoration, thanksgiving and confession, and even of instruction; thus were the laws concerning the sacrifices daily recited, with the hope and prayer that God would soon reinstate them.

"Prayer" was recited from memory for many years. It was not until 875 A.D. that the "Gaon" Amram undertook the task of definitely prescribing the ritual for the various services. But even after his time, there were many additions of liturgic poems to be recited on certain holy days. However, these additions were not obligatory.

This compilation of prayers — "Siddur" — was generally accepted as the authorized prayerbook. A radical change in liturgy was later instituted by the Reformists. They dropped many of the age-old hallowed prayers, in particular all those which have to do with the return of Zion and the ancient sacrificial rites. They introduced the sermon as a fixed factor of the service while previously it had been used only occasionally.

They also began to use the language of their country for the prayers instead of Hebrew which had been used for prayer all through the ages with few exceptions. (Some prayers are in Aramaic.)

THE THREE DAILY PRAYERS

The custom of praying three times a day has its roots in antiquity. Psalm 55:17 tells of praying evening, morning and noon. Daniel (6:10, 11) also prayed three times a day. The morning prayer (shacharith) lasts about an hour. The afternoon (mincha) and evening (ma'ariv) services are usually one following the other and together they, too, last about one hour.

Besides the three daily prayers at the synagogue, there is also

---

[4] The "Shema" is the most solemn "prayer" (recited three times daily) and consists of the verses of Deuteronomy 6:4-9, 13-21 and Numbers 15:37-41. It is, particularly the first part of it, a profession of faith in and dedication to God (the One and only God) — the quintessence of Judaism.

some reading, during the service, in the sacred scroll of the Pentateuch, on Mondays and Thursdays. During the Sabbath service a whole "sidra" (see vocabulary) is read from the Pentateuch, to which was added a portion from the "Prophets." There are also additions to the usual daily prayers — on the Sabbath and holy-days. (The Rosh Hashonah service lasts several hours, while that of Yom Kippur lasts a whole day and a great part of the preceding night.)

The additions to the morning service on holy days are mostly "piutim," poetical compositions, incorporated during the Middle Ages, some of which are devotional, some doctrinal or dealing with Law, or even allusions to some historical event.

We cannot within the limited space of this book enlarge upon the various "prayers" or rather parts of these prayers, and we would therefore advise the student to procure a Jewish prayerbook in English translation and study it. It would be well worthwhile.

PREPARATION AND POSTURE

Prayer requires preparation. It needs dedication and purification of mind and body. The worshiper must exclude all worldly and selfish thoughts while in communication with the Creator. Also his body must be clean. No one may pray or utter the name of God without previously washing his hands. Pious Jews used to wash the whole body by immersion in a ritual basin (Mikveh) before the morning prayer. The lower part of the body was considered as not clean enough for prayer, so a special belt is worn during prayer to separate it from the upper part which does the actual performance of the ritual.

The morning prayer (scharith) is to be recited in a "tallith" (a praying-shawl), and "tefillin" (phylacteries). These are not used on Sabbath nor on Holy Days.

The solemn prayers are recited in standing posture, facing the East — in the direction of Jerusalem, according to I Kings 8:38; II Chronicles 6:39. So we find Daniel (6:10, 11) praying three times daily with his face turned toward Jerusalem. At home a picture called "Mizrach" (east) hung on the wall facing the East as a reminder of the location of Jerusalem. In the synagogue, the "east wall" has special importance: there stands the ark containing the Torah and there are the seats of the rabbi and the other dignitaries of the community.

While the prayers may be recited alone at home, the recitation is better and more efficacious when done in a congregation because the "Shekinah" is present when ten or more Jews are united in prayer. This quorum of ten (minyan) must be adult males over thirteen years of age. When a Jewish boy reaches the age of thirteen he becomes "Bar-Mitzvah" (a son of the Law) — responsible to Law, and a full-fledged member of the Jewish community with all religious duties and privileges that this entails.

When the service is performed in "congregation," one of the congregants (if over thirteen years old) serves as leader called "Chazan" (see vocabulary) cantor, or "Baal Tefillah" ("man of prayer").

While any one of the congregation may perform all the rites in the service, larger congregations have special functionaries for leading in prayer, reading in the Scrolls, blowing of the Shofar, etc. Only the Priestly benediction may not be performed by a layman. It must be done by descendants of Aaron, the first priest.

The Benediction that follows the larger meals is quite elaborate and is also better performed by a quorum of three, at least, of whom one is the leader. In the singing of "Zemiroth" which accompanies the meals on Sabbath and holy days, all the male household participate.

As already mentioned all prayers, with little exception, are recited in Hebrew, although not many of those who recite the prayers understand them.

CHAPTER VI

THE JEWISH COMMUNITY — (K'HILLAH)

A. THE SYNAGOGUE

This institution is well known in the New Testament. It originated during the vacant period between the Old Testament and
the New Testament. While the Temple existed this was only a
supplement to the service in the Temple. There in the synagogue
the people could meet for prayer, study of the Law and probably
also for discussion about communal and national affairs.[1] After
the destruction of the Temple and the cessation of the sacrificial
service the synagogue became the center of worship and of Jewish
life as a whole. It was from the synagogue in diaspora that Paul
disseminated the Gospel to the Jew first and also to the Gentile.

Now, like the Jewish religious life in general so also the synagogue is on a sharp decline, but until quite recently (before the
two world wars) the synagogue in the old Jewish communities was
the center and circumference of Jewish life. It was the treasury of
Jewish ideals, doctrines and history. There the Jews, almost all the
males, met day by day for the three daily services. There Jews,
individually or in groups, spent most of the day and a great portion of the night in study of the sacred books — and most synagogues usually had large libraries of sacred books placed on shelves
free for all. That is why the synagogue is also called in Yiddish
shool (school), because it was there that the Jew got his "Judaism," and, as already mentioned, Judaism to him meant life — as
it controlled almost all his thoughts and actions. The Greek word
synagogue is a translation of the Hebrew word *beth-knesseth*
which means the House of Assembly (or congregation). Any Jew

[1] There were 460 synagogues in Jerusalem in the time of Christ (according
to the Talmud). Jesus frequented the synagogues of His home town, Nazareth,
also in Capernaum and others as is recorded in Matthew 12:9; Luke 4:16;
John 6:59; 18:20. Paul preached the Gospel in the synagogues as seen in
Acts 13:5; 14:1; 18:4.

could come in at any time of day or night (not during service) for a rest, a chat or even a nap. It was his club, a second home.

The Christian missionary is advised to attend some Jewish services at the synagogue and get acquainted with the order of service and also with the things inside the edifice. The most sacred part in the synagogue is the "Ark," reminiscent of the "Ark of the Covenant," usually called *"Aron Hakodesh"* (the Holy Ark) wherein the "Sepher Torah" is kept. This Torah is a parchment scroll on which the "Five Books of Moses" are written by hand in the original Hebrew text. The Ark is placed in a recess in the east wall. Its doors are covered by a curtain called *parachet*. In front of it is usually suspended a *ner tamid* — a perpetual lamp, always lighted. In about the center of the synagogue stands the *Bema,* (which may be translated as "pulpit"), upon which the Sepher Torah is laid when it is read. In many synagogues the Bema serves also as a platform at which the Chazan (cantor) stands when leading in prayer. There also stands the Rabbi when he delivers a sermon. Some synagogues have a special "stand," at which the man leading in prayer stands.

Some striking features about the synagogues are: The absence of pictorial emblems (no portraits or statues). No instrumental music is allowed (Reform Temples are exceptions in this regard), and conspicuous by their absence are the women. No women are allowed inside the prayer hall. Those women who want to pray (although women are not enjoined to recite prayers) with the congregation, may do so in an adjoining room. Some synagogues have balconies for the women. In Reform Temples there is mixed seating. You may know that one of the benedictions in the morning service is: "Blessed art thou . . . who has not made me a woman."

B. The Functionaries of the Synagogue

The Functionaries of the Synagogue or of the community, as a whole, are usually composed of:

1. *The* "Rabbi." Formerly his most important duties were to care for the religious needs of his congregation, especially see to it that the community is provided with *kosher* food (see Vocabulary). Under his jurisdiction came also the laws and rites of marriage and divorce. (These *kosher* and marital laws are also the main tasks of the Israeli Rabbinate). Today, and particularly in Western countries (U. S. A., England, France, etc.), the rabbis, especially the Reform rabbis (imitation of the Christian pastor), have assumed many of the modern pastor's activities: as preaching

sermons, sometimes also leading in prayer, and certain social activities. He is expected to be a good "mixer" and he is so usually, "a jolly good fellow."

2. *The* "Shochet" ("slaughterer"), who in a prescribed manner slaughters *kosher* (ritually fit) animals, mainly chicken and cattle, and thus is supplying *kosher* meat for the Jewish consumer.

3. *The* "Chazan" (cantor), who leads in the service; sometimes he also serves as the *"baal korei"* (Reader from the scroll of the Torah) although these two offices may be, and it often has been, performed by anyone of the congregants who volunteers for them.

4. *The* "Mohel" — the circumciser.

5. *The* "Sofeir," a scribe who writes the "Torah," (here meaning "the five books of Moses," which for synagogual use are to be written by hand on parchment). He also writes on parchment the passages from the Pentateuch that are enclosed in the *tefillin*, (phylacteries) and in the *mezuzzah* (small scroll nailed to the door post). Smaller communities which cannot support a *sofeir* of their own import their religious articles from other communities.

6. *The* "Gabbai," or Treasurer, one of whose tasks is to allot the various duties or "treats" connected with the service.

7. *The* "Shamash," who serves as beadle, sexton and usher as the occasion may require. Up to a generation or two ago, the Shamash had the task of calling the Jews to the synagogue to pray. Thus, before dawn he used to go around the Jewish sections of the towns with a hammer knocking on the doors or shutters, crying aloud: "Get up, get up to the service of the Creator." On Fridays, in the late afternoon, he used to go about crying: "To synagogue!" ("In shul arein!"). This was an indication to all those laggards who were not yet ready for the Sabbath, to hurry up, wash and dress fittingly and rush to the Synagogue. The Shamash also served as the Rabbi's messenger in his function as Rabbi.

C. Mikveh

Every community has had a *Mikveh* — a bath for ritual ablution and immersion for purification, mainly for women after the period of their menstruation (only after she had performed this cleansing ritual was she considered as "clean"). The males used it for cleansing their bodies on the eve of Sabbath, and on holy days. Some pious Jews purified themselves in the Mikveh every morning in preparation for Prayer.

D. OTHER INSTITUTIONS

Since the synagogue had been the center of Jewish life, there clustered about it various associations for the spiritual and temporal welfare of the individual Jew as well as for the community as a whole. There was the *chevrah kadisha* (the sacred Association) whose task had been to care for the ritual of the dead, and the upkeep of the cemetery. There were societies for the care of the sick, the aged, the orphaned, helping poor brides to get married, to provide the poor with "Matzeth" (unleavened bread) and wine for the Passover, to provide lodging for strangers, to buy books (sacred) for the library and many others. There were various groups for study; groups to study the Talmudic books with all their hair-splitting casuistry and intricacies. Less learned folk (and with less time at their disposal) joined themselves into *Mishnah* groups. The Mishnah was written in Hebrew, and is not so difficult and intricate as is the *Gemarah* which is mostly in Aramaic. And there was the *Ain Yaakov* group. This book contains, in simple Hebrew, the homiletical portions of the Talmudic books and their various legends. The less learned people, usually the busy working men, satisfied themselves with the reading of the Psalms in spare time.

As a whole the synagogue and its services have been the expression of the common hopes and yearnings, of the ideals, exultations, joys and sorrows of the Jewish people. To be expelled from the synagogue was considered a most terrible punishment (see John 9:22; 12:42).

In conclusion, I wish to emphasize again that the synagogue, as all Judaism, is rapidly losing its grip on the Jewish people. It is becoming less and less a force in Jewry.

In America where the largest number of the Jewish people is settled, imposing synagogues are erected, but they are no longer "houses of prayer" and inspiration. Their purpose seems to be more negative than positive. It is more to keep the Jews away from the influence of the Christians, than to teach them Judaism. For fear that the Jewish youth might stray away into Gentile society, everything is being done to attract them to a place where they could keep to themselves. Thus the synagogue is rapidly becoming a social center with sports, dances, and various other entertainments. No inducement is spared to keep the adolescent within the fold and dissuade him from inter-marriage and assimilation.

The Reform Jews call their religious center a "Temple" — a

word which to the modern liberal ear sounds better than the word "synagogue," because, although the word is of non-Jewish origin, the institution itself is uniquely (and peculiarly) Jewish. The Liberal Reform Jews prefer not to be stamped and identified as Jews (they prefer some degree of painless assimilation).

CHAPTER VII

FEASTS AND FASTS

THE JEWISH CALENDAR

The Jewish people count the year "to the creation of the world," which according to tradition and based on biblical data occurred 5720 years ago. Thus the year 1961-1962 is in the Jewish year 5722. This reckoning *"to the creation"* is not mentioned in the Bible. Instead, the Bible era especially in regard to the festive seasons, is *"to the going out of Egypt."* Thus the Jews have two systems of reckoning the years: 1. the Sacred year which begins in Spring in memory of *"the going out of Egypt"* and 2. the Civil (or secular) year which begins in Autumn when the *"world was created."* For example, the feast of Passover is celebrated in the *first* Sacred month (Nisan), "This month shall be unto you the beginning of months: it shall be the first month of the year to you" (Exodus 12:2), while what the Jews call *"New Year"* (the Bible calls the "Memorial of Blowing of Trumpets"; see Leviticus 23:24 and Numbers 10:10; 29:1) is celebrated on the first day of the *seventh* Sacred month.

The year is divided into twelve lunar months (of 29½ days) with a 13th month seven times in every cycle of nineteen years. The lunar year (12 times 29½ days) has 354 days, and is thus eleven days shorter than the solar year, which counts 365 days. In order to make up for this annual difference, a whole month is inserted every third or second year. Thus every 3rd, 6th, 8th, 11th, 14th, 17th, and 19th year (in a cycle of 19 years) is a leap year of 13 months. The months do not have 29½ days each but alternate in length: Nisan has 30 days, Iyar 29 days, and so on. In some years there is a little variation in the length of the months for certain reasons.

The names of the Jewish months are not given in Hebrew in the Bible. The Jews learned them from the people in Babylon during their exile in that country. In the Bible the months are usually named by ordinal numbers (1st month, 2nd month, etc.).

Nor are there Hebrew names for the days of the week. The names of the days and months used by Christians are of pagan origin! The names of the Jewish months are: 1. *Nisan* (corresponds to March 20 up to April 16 or thereabouts), 2. *Iyar*, 3. *Sivan*, 4. *Tammuz*, 5. *Av*, 6. *Elul*, 7. *Tishri*, 8. *Cheshvan*, 9. *Kislev*, 10. *Teveth*, 11. *Shevat*, 12. *Adar*. In a leap year the 13th month is called *Ve-Adar*.

The present Jewish Calendar is based on astronomical principles and was adopted about 1500 years ago. Before its adoption (as in the time of Christ), the Rabbis did not rely on scientific calculations. They were probably not well acquainted with astronomical rules, and their chief reliance was on actual observation of the moon. On the thirtieth day of each month the Rabbis (during the Second Temple — The Sanhedrin) examined witnesses who claimed to have seen the *new moon*. If the evidence was reliable and satisfactory, that day (the 30th) was formally proclaimed to be "New Moon" *(Rosh Chodesh)*. If there were no witnesses, or the evidence was not trustworthy, the month was declared to begin on the following day. Since upon the date of the *New Moon* depended the date of any festival that fell in the month, the people all over the country were informed by messengers or by beacon signals from mountain tops of this formal *"sanctification of the New Month."* Those Jews who lived too far away from Jerusalem to be reached in time, and thus could not know whether the 30th day was declared as New Moon, had to keep sacred both the 30th day as well as the following day, and accordingly every festival of that month had to be kept two days instead of one day as it was observed in the homeland. "New Years' Day" was celebrated for two days even in Jerusalem, because it fell on the first day of the month. The adoption of the "Second Day Festival" is still being observed in Diaspora (outside Israel) although the exact time of the appearance of the new moon is now well known and is printed in the Jewish Calendar. Thus, for example, Shavuoth — Pentecost — is kept two days instead of one day as fixed in the Bible.

Holy Days

Before continuing here, it is important to'read carefully concerning the biblical festive seasons in Leviticus, chapter 23 and Numbers, chapters 28 and 29.

I would call the reader's attention to the fact that my portrayal of the various holydays here is as they have been observed in the diaspora up to three or four decades ago and as I knew them in my early youth. Today, especially in America, the holydays have no longer the great significance, the ennobling effect upon Jewry they had previously. If any of them are observed at all, it is less in compliance with the Word of God, than it is in compliance with men, especially with old parents; some dim and vague nostalgia; and more often than not to hear the voice of a "famous Chazan," or Cantor who sings and recites the prayers in enchanting tones. Sometimes the sermon or rather "lecture" of the learned Rabbi draws attendance to the synagogues and temples on the holydays, especially on "New Year" and on the "Day of Atonement."

Since the destruction of the Temple and cessation of Sacrifices the holydays were not celebrated in exile in accordance with the Word of God. For example:

1. According to the Scriptures the holydays were to be celebrated by various offerings. In exile there were no sacrifices.

2. The ritual service of "Day of Atonement" was mainly performed by the priests as it was a sacrificial ministry, whereas the people as a whole had almost nothing to do with it except to keep it holy like a Sabbath Day and to fast.[1] In Diaspora this day has become the most important day in the observance of the Jewish Religion.

3. *"New Year"* which together with the "Day of Atonement" has become known as the "awful days" (when even those Jews who don't usually attend the synagogue find it obligatory to attend) is not mentioned in the Scriptures at all.

4. According to the Scriptures the "First Day of the Month" was to be a solemn holyday; while in exile, and especially now, it had little importance.

5. I may add that while God ordained the holydays to be kept only one day, in exile they were kept two days. Only *Yom Kippur* is observed one day.

There have been many other discrepancies in the observance of the holydays in variance with the Scriptures.

However, bereft of the possibility of offering the prescribed sacrifices, the Jews did in their own way, keep the holydays "holy" in the highest possible degree. Here again we may use Paul's words, "Zeal without knowledge," but such well-meant zeal, such devotion, such submission in love, awe and reverence to God as the Jews evidence in their holydays may well have earned them

[1] The Hebrew words for "ye shall afflict your souls" (see Leviticus 16:31; 23:23; Numbers 29:7) is generally understood to mean "to fast."

the name of "God's Chosen People." That bears true witness to Israel's potentialities to fulfill their mission at the close of the "times of the Gentiles."

SABBATH

Keeping the Sabbath holy is one of the Ten Commandments (See Exodus 20:8-11; Deuteronomy 5:12-15). The Sabbath has been the center of Jewish life and of the Jewish home. No matter how badly the Jew fared during weekdays, on the Sabbath he was his own self — a scion of kings and prophets. No matter what his position was within the community, no matter if through the weekdays he and his family suffered the pangs of hunger and other adversities of poverty; no matter how he was despised or beaten and bruised by non-Jews from without, when the Sabbath came he was transformed into a king — at least as lord and master of his home.

In the old ghetto life and within the Jewish settlement, it seemed that the six weekdays were only days of preparation for the proper observance of the Sabbath. Friday was almost entirely devoted to preparation for the advent of holy Sabbath: baking, cooking, housecleaning, everything was done (no cost was spared) that the home, no matter how dingy and congested, should be converted into a royal abode. While the menfolk went to have the ritual cleansing at the Mikveh, the community bath, the women-folk washed themselves at home. All put on the cleanest and best clothing, usually special "Sabbath-clothing." Toward evening the men went to the synagogue for "Reception of Sabbath," as the Sabbath-eve service is called where special prayers and chants were recited and sung. The center of the service is the beautiful hymn called *L'cha Dodi*, "Come My Beloved," which clearly hints that the Messiah is already come.

When the men return from synagogue they find their home (perhaps simply a one-room home) highly illuminated, especially with Sabbath candles, the table being festively decked with the best that their income can afford. On entering, the men greet the women, *"Gut shabbes"* ("Have a good Sabbath") and all reply, *"Gut shabbes."* Then everyone chants a welcoming song in honor of the two angels, who are believed to accompany every man home from his Sabbath-eve service.

Then comes the *Kiddush* (sanctification) which the head of the family solemnly pronounces over a cup of wine of which every-one tastes after the blessing. Then after washing of hands the whole family, "king" father, "queen" mother and the other members of "royalty" sit down around the table, happily, radiantly partaking of the delicious food, interspersed with *Zmiroth* — sacred songs — which terminate with the final lengthy blessing.

The following day is consecrated entirely to the service of God. There is the morning service at the synagogue which occupies almost all of the forenoon, then the festive meal which, with its accompanying prayers and chants is also considered as part of the divine service.

The afternoon is spent in reading sacred books; each according to his education. Then again to synagogue for the late afternoon service and a third meal, a light one, after which, at nightfall, there comes the daily evening service.

The Sabbath is then terminated by *Havdalah* ("separation"). Like the *Kiddush* which ushers in the holy day, so also the *Havdalah*, which separates the sacred Sabbath from the secular weekdays, is performed over a cup of wine. Then comes *M'lavesh Malkah* — a farewell meal in honor of the departing queen — Sabbath. This meal accompanied by recitations and chants often lasts till late at night.

The Sabbath had to be observed not only by observing affirmative laws, in special prayers, rites and ceremonial meals, but also by refraining from doing certain things. The Bible forbids doing work on the Sabbath day, but it does not say exactly what is to be considered as work. So the Rabbis wrote down hundreds of acts which are to be considered as work. Certain objects which may lead to the desecration of the Sabbath, such as money, candles, etc., should not even be touched. No burden ought to be carried on the Sabbath. Pious Jews even refrain from carrying a handkerchief, though in case of necessity it was wound around the neck like a scarf and was considered as a garment. No fire is to be kindled on the Sabbath ("Ye shall kindle no fire throughout your habitations upon the Sabbath day," Exodus 35:3), so the Jews (in exile) had to use the service of a Gentile to make a fire in the stove in cold weather, also to remove the candlesticks from the table, when not in use.

Present day Orthodox Jews refrain from turning on electric lights, even from using the telephone, radio and television sets, since a spark is lit when activating them. Nor may a burning light or fire be extinguished. Thus some Jews kindle their lights before Sabbath sets in, and let them burn till the Sabbath is out. Others use various gadgets which automatically turn on and off the electric current.

Smoking tobacco on the Sabbath is strictly prohibited. Prohibited, too, is riding, either on an animal or on a vehicle. Only when on board ship may the Jew continue his voyage on the Sabbath. Jews of old, and observant Jews now, have been cautious not to break any of the hundreds of Sabbath laws. Yet in spite of these harsh limitations (so many "don'ts"), the day was not only a holy day but also a day of delight, of joy and happiness. The Jew excluded all worry, sorrow, and mourning and, of course, all thoughts of any part of his weekday occupation.

Well was it said by a Jewish sage: "More than the Jews kept the Sabbath has the Sabbath kept the Jews." They surely could not have survived the everyday hardships, if they had not had the weekly day of rest and resuscitation, a day on which they could remind themselves that they are the "Everlasting Nation," the nation who had a Covenant with God.

The other holydays, too, were kept as holy as humanly possible. They have been days fully consecrated to God. No sports or any kind of entertainment were allowed — only prayer, study of sacred books, and consumption of food eaten solemnly and ritually.

THE THREE PILGRIM FESTIVALS

"Three times a year shall all thy males appear before the Lord thy God in the place which he shall choose, in the feast of unleavened bread, and in the feast of weeks, and in the feast of tabernacles: and they shall not appear before the Lord empty" (Deuteronomy 16:16): 1. *Pesach* (Passover); 2. *Shavuoth* (Weeks); 3. *Succoth* (Tabernacles).

According to the Bible the first and seventh days of Passover, the day of Pentecost, and the first and eighth days of Tabernacles were to be kept as "holy assemblies" (Lev. 23). In the Diaspora, an additional day is observed in each case (see Section on Jewish Calendar). The day after each of the three Pilgrim Festivals is called *Isru Chag*, which is a kind of a half-holiday.

I. PESACH (Passover)

Most interesting volumes have been written on this Festival.[2] We here must limit ourselves to some of the main points. The name Passover refers to Exodus 12:27, and is celebrated for eight days (in Israel only seven) from the 15th of Nisan to the 22nd of Nisan — the first month of the Jewish Year. The first two days

[2] The author has published a book on Passover from the Christian viewpoint.

and the last two days are full holydays, while the intervening days are half-holidays ("Chol-haMoed"), when work may be done.

Passover is also called Feast of *Matzoth* (Unleavened Bread)[3] and *Feast of Harvest*, because this falls at the time of the barley harvest. As thanksgiving for the harvest, an *omer* (a certain measure of the new grain) had to be offered on the second day of Passover. (About *Pesach* read also Matthew 26:17-19; Luke 22:7-20; I Corinthians 5:7, 8; 6:7; 11:24-26.)

The most festive and ceremonious part of Passover is the *Seder*, the ritual meal or "home service" of the first two nights of Passover. Even more than the Sabbath eve, the home looks as if magically converted into a royal hall. Light, joy and happiness permeate the atmosphere. While on Sabbath eve the head of the family assumes the role of a King, on the Eve of Passover he is more of a "high priest," and the table around which the family is seated is more like an altar, as it is decked with sacred symbols, each of which commemorates some particular event of the deliverance from Egypt. The table-service begins with the Kiddush (as on Sabbath eve). It is continued with reciting the *Haggadah* — the story of the miraculous deliverance. The recitation and chanting of the various parts of the Haggadah (some of which are devotional, others quite frivolous) together with the ritual food, often occupy the greater part of the night.

While most of this home service is a memorial to the redemption from Egyptian slavery, there are also many symbols pointing at the redemption of the soul by the Messiah, and the mystery of the Trinity. Such, for example, are the *three Mazzoth*, the bone of a lamb, the *Aphikomen*, and the "Cup of wine for Elijah."[4]

When and how these apparently Christian symbols got into the Passover ceremony is not yet very clear. The Jews who solemnly observe them have no good explanation for this.

At the services of the synagogue during Passover, special prayers are added to the daily ones. Also certain sections of the Torah, relevant to this holiday are being read.

Sephirah ("counting"), or the Counting of the Omer. We have previously mentioned the offering of the "Omer." Now the Bible commanded to count seven weeks from that day till the Offering of the *First Fruit (Bikkurim)* on the fiftieth day. (See Leviticus 23:15-17; Exodus 34:22; Numbers 28:26.)

---

[3] Because no bread other than unleavened may be eaten during the eight days of Passover (see Exodus 12:19, 20; 13:7; 18:18).

[4] See my book on Passover for particulars.

In Exile these days of Sephirah assumed a new phase: They have been considered as days of mourning (no weddings or other joyous celebrations on these days). Various reasons are given for it (see further on *Lag-baomer*), but none is better than that it originated from the time that the first Christians mourned over the crucifixion of Jesus till His reappearance and reassurance on the fiftieth day — on *Pentecost*. This is my opinion.

SHAVUOTH (Weeks) — The Feast of Weeks
(See Exodus 34:22; Leviticus 23:15-17; also read
Acts chapter 2, and I Corinthians 15:20.)

It is celebrated on the sixth and seventh day of the month of *Sivan* — the third month of the year. To Christians it is known as *Pentecost,* a Greek word which means "fiftieth" — the fiftieth day after the bringing of the Omer. In biblical times it was also called *The Festival of the Wheat Harvest.* (Two loaves were offered from the new crop.) It was also called *The Day of First Fruit.* From this day until *Succoth* (the third Pilgrim Festival) the first fruits of the field (wheat, grapes, figs, pomegranates, olives, etc.) were brought by the Jewish farmers to the Temple as a token of gratitude to the Lord for His bounty (see Deuteronomy 26:5).

In Exile, Shavuoth lost its biblical character (which was agricultural and sacerdotal). It has become the *Feast of the Giving of Our Law,* as according to tradition, on this day occurred the Revelation on Mount Sinai, when the Torah was entrusted to the People of Israel (see Exodus 19:1).

(Significant about the special synagogue service is the reading of the book of Ruth, the Moabite woman of whom sprang the royal family of David — and the Messiah.)

III. SUCCOTH (Tabernacles)
(Leviticus 23:34-43; Deuteronomy 16:13-16)

This commences on the fifteenth of *Tishri,* the seventh month of the year, and ends on the twenty-third of that month. It is also called *The Festival of the Ingathering* (see Exodus 34:22). The special feature of this Festival is that meals are eaten in specially built booths (the very pious even sleep in them). Another important feature is the observance of the "four species," in accordance with Leviticus 23:40; "And ye shall take you on the first day the boughs of goodly trees, branches of palm trees, and the boughs of thick trees, and willows of the brook; and ye shall rejoice before the Lord your God seven days."

The seventh day of Succoth is called *Hoshana Rabba,* and the eighth day is *Shemini Atzereth* (Leviticus 23:36). The ninth day is *Simchath Torah* ("Rejoicing of the Law"). In Palestine, this holyday is celebrated on the eighth day together with Shemini Atzereth. This festival has no basis in the Bible. On this day the annual reading of the Torah[5] is completed and recommenced for the coming year.

This is a very joyful day. In the synagogue during service all the sacred scrolls are taken out of the Holy Ark, and carried by young and old in procession. Children also partake in the reading of the Torah.

(Women may be present in a secluded part of the synagogue during the services — but they never participate.)

THE FEARFUL DAYS

I. ROSH HASHANAH *(New Year).* This holyday falls on the first and second day of the *seventh month — Tishri.* Among the order of the sacrifices for each holyday enumerated in Numbers 28 and 29, there are also special sacrifices to be offered on the first day of the seventh month, which more than other New Moons was to be kept holy (see Numbers 29:1-6). (The number "7" had some symbolic significance in the Bible [in Hebrew lore], thus also the 7th day of the week, the 7th year, etc. had special significance.)

This *seventh* New Moon was, somehow, in Exile, converted into the *New Year* and the *Yom Haddin* — "The Day of Judgment," when God sits in judgment of each and every creature and decides the fate of each in the following year. But the sealing of the judgment is done on the tenth day of Tishri — the Day of Atonement. In the intervening time man can still repent and repair any wrong he had committed during the past year. The two days of "New Year" and the Day of Atonement are called "The Fearful Days," and together with the seven intervening days, are called "The Ten Days of Repentance," when by prayer, alms-giving and fasting one may avert the execution of the deserved penalties.

Thus before Rosh Hashanah is over Jews greet each other with the earnest wish, "May you be inscribed to a good year." Between Rosh Hashanah and Day of Atonement the greeting is, "May you be sealed to a good year." "Inscribed," of course, refers into the "Book of Life." There is not much festivity at home on

[5] The Torah (Pentateuch) is being read in the synagogue on Sabbaths in about fifty weekly portions until it is all read over the period of the year.

Rosh Hashanah. On the other hand, the services at the synagogue are very elaborate, including many prayers for forgiveness and the blowing of the SHOFAR (horn) (see Numbers 29:1 and Leviticus 23:24). Another solemn feature is the reading of the story of the Sacrifice of Isaac in Genesis 22, as a reminder to God to remember the covenant and forgive for Isaac's sake.

II. YOM KIPPUR (Day of Atonement) — (See Leviticus 16:30 and Numbers 29:7)

This is the most solemn day in the Jewish year. It is a total fast day which begins with the preceding evening. Not even a drop of water may be taken into the mouth. All the day as well as a great part of the previous night is spent in the synagogue. Solemn and touching is the commencing service (called *Kol Nidre*) on the eve of Yom Kippur and the concluding service (called *Neilah*).

On the day before Yom Kippur the rite of *Kapparah* is performed. Since the person who sins deserves to die and since there is no man without sin, and since the ordained sacrifices have ceased, the people take a substitute which is to die as a ransom. Usually the male takes a cock, and the female, a hen, and by reciting certain prayers and circling the fowl around the penitent's head, it takes over the sins and accordingly is to die instead of the human. This "sacrifice" is then ritually slaughtered and consumed or given to the poor and needy. This rite is now seldom practiced. Only the extremely pious still cling to it.

This rite as well as the other rituals, prayer, fasting and charity does not allay the sense of guilt, does not dispel the fear of just retribution; somehow they fear that all these are not enough for atonement. It is no wonder that they call these days "Fearful."

Is it not our duty to tell them of the Lamb of God, of the great Sacrifice made for the Atonement of all that believe on Him?

THE MINOR FESTIVALS

I. CHANUCAH (Dedication) — This festival is celebrated for eight days beginning from the 25th of Kislev (the ninth month). It commemorates the re-dedication of the Temple by the Maccabees. The events that led to this festival are recorded in the Apocryphal Book of "Maccabees." In short: the "Greeks" (here, actually the Syrians) intended to subdue the small state of Judea and force the Jews to abandon Judaism and instead to adopt the worship of Greek gods. While all the nations around· (in the near East) yielded to this superior power, the Jews, faithful to Jehovah (God) revolted, defeated the mighty armies of the idolatrous enemy (in

165 B.C) and rededicated the Temple which had then been defiled and desecrated by the "Hellenists."

The Kindling of the Chanucah Lights commemorates the miracle which took place at the rededication. The Talmud tells that when the victorious Maccabees were seeking the sacred oil to rekindle the "Menorah" (the continual lamp — see Exodus 27:20), they found only one cruse of oil, whose seal of the High Priest was unbroken, and was thus undefiled. This sacred oil was sufficient only for one day; yet, miraculously it lasted for eight days.

There is no special sanctity to this holiday except that certain prayers are added to the daily prayers, and that in the evening the Chanucah candles are solemnly lit, accompanied with benedictions and recitations. It is considered more of a children's holiday, as they have usually been free from school and received gifts from the adults. There is no limitation on work.

John, the Evangelist, tells (John 10:22-39) of Jesus being at the Temple on Chanucah, when the people who were, at that time, expecting the Messiah, asked Him if He was the Messiah.

It is quite possible that the early Christians celebrated this *Feast of Lights* (as Chanucah is often called) and in course of time, after the marvelous widespread 'influx of Gentiles into the Christian faith, it evolved into a new holyday — what we now call Christmas.

(Let us pray for the time when both Jew and Gentile will together celebrate the *Feast of the Light of the World*.)

II. PURIM (Lots), falls on the 14th and 15th of Adar, the 12th month. In English it is called the *Feast of Esther*, as its origin is in the book of Esther. The Jews call it "Lots" (see Esther 9: 26-32).

It is celebrated in commemoration of the deliverance of the Jewish people in Persia about 23 centuries ago. Like Chanucah, work may be done on the two days of Purim. The services in the synagogue are distinguished by the reading of the *Book of Esther*, and at home by festive meals. This is a merry holiday when Jews are allowed to get drunk, to masquerade and even to ridicule the Rabbis, and to distort and recite certain prayers to make them sound ridiculous, and thus arouse laughter.

The children are given license to raise as much noise as they wish. In the synagogue whenever the name Haman is read during the reading of the *Megillah* ("Scroll": Book of Esther), the children make noise by specially fabricated noisemakers, whistles, fire crackers, etc.

Haman (as you may know) was the first modern anti-Semite who about 23 centuries ago declared that the Jews ought to be exterminated because they are different from all other nations. ("And Haman said unto king Ahasuerus, There is a certain people scattered abroad and dispersed among the people in all the provinces of thy kingdom; and their laws are diverse from all people; neither keep they the king's laws; therefore it is not for the king's profit to suffer them" — Esther 3:8.)

Haman and many others after him, have endeavored to destroy the Jewish people, but they survived, because "No weapon that is formed against thee shall prosper," Isaiah 54:17, because they are indestructible — an everlasting nation.

The most welcome part of this holiday is, of course, the sending of gifts to friends and to the poor.

There are two remarkable things about this Festival:

1. The book of Esther (upon which the festival is based) is the only book in the Bible wherein not even once is mentioned the name of God in any form, although the hand of God is felt on every page of it.

2. The Talmud says that all the festivals will be abolished when Messiah comes, only this festival, PURIM, will remain. This is the only festival mentioned in the Bible which God did *not* command. In Esther 9:20-28 it states that Mordecai wrote to the Jews to observe this festival, and that the Jews took it upon themselves and upon their children to observe it forever. Also, Esther wrote an edict to all the Jews — to the same effect.

On whose authority? Has God approved of it? (There is some mystery in this — and someday we may be privileged to know it).

III. ROSH CHODESH (literally: The Head of the Month)

In pre-exile time the first day of each month was solemnly celebrated and additional sacrifices were offered (see Numbers 28:11-31). From II Kings 4:23, we understand that it was an established festival. And Amos 8:5 seems to indicate that no work was allowed on Rosh Chodesh. In course of time it lost its importance. Now it is almost forgotten except that additional prayers are recited on this day.

IV. LAG BAOMER

The 33rd day of the Counting of the Omer (see Pesach) is a half-holiday. The origin of this holiday is obscure. Formerly it was ascribed to a plague which occurred in Judea (about 70 A.D.)

during the days of the SEPHIRA (see Pesach), but on this day the plague stopped. Now it is ascribed to the revolt of the false Messiah Bar Kochba which terminated with a horrible massacre and the final cessation of Jewish life in Judea. (In that case, why celebrate?)

There is no special service on this day. Children are free from school, and they play as "soldiers." In the land of Israel bon-fires are made at night, the youngsters dancing and singing around them. Many of the pious visit the sepulchre of Rabbi Shimon Bar Yochai, at Meron near Saffad (in Upper Galilee). This Rabbi was (according to popular tradition) a great Kabbalist and miracle man, and even the mere visit to his grave may bring the fulfillment of wishes, according to popular belief. Here great illuminations are made accompanied with prayer and chants. Many people from far and wide also visit the sepulchre of Rabbi Akiba at Tiberias, who was one of the most revered Rabbis (he may have known Jesus, but later was the sponsor of Bar Kochba).

V. Tu B'SHVATH (or Chamishäh-Assar Beshvat)

The fifteenth day of the SHVAT (the eleventh month), is also called "The New Year of Trees." In pre-exile times this day was considered as the agricultural New Year in regard to tithes and the like. In Exile the day was celebrated by eating various fruits, preferably such as grow in Palestine (figs, dates, almonds, etc.).

In the land of Israel, now, Tu B'SHVAT is celebrated by planting of new trees, in towns and villages or new forests, recalling the words of the Bible: "When you come into the land you shall plant all kinds of trees . . ." (Leviticus 19:23).

The 15th of Av was a holiday in the times of the Second Temple. It is not now observed.

FAST DAYS

Besides *Yom Kippur* which is the only fast commanded by God[6], there are five other fast-days:

I. TISHAH B'AV (the ninth day of Av — the fifth month). This is a very strict fast and like the fast of "Yom Kippur" it begins with the previous evening. It is a day of deep mourning as on this day the First Temple as well as the second one was destroyed. The Book of Lamentation is recited at the synagogue which is but dimly lighted while the worshipers sit or squat on the floor, a

6 See note on page 75.

token of mourning. A book called *Kinnoth,* a collection of Laments and Wailings is chanted, with sighing and weeping and groaning.

II. SHIVAH ASSAR B'TAMMUZ (the 17th day of Tammuz — the fourth month), commemorating the capture of Jerusalem and siege of the Second Temple by the Romans.

The "Three Weeks" intervening between this fast and "Tishah B'av," are weeks of mourning. No wedding or any other joyous occasion is allowed.

III. ZOM G'DALYAH (The Fast of G'dalyah) commemorates the murder of the governor of the Jews who was appointed by Nebuchadnezzar (see II Kings 25:25). The fast falls on the day next to Rosh Hashanah (the 3rd of Tishri).

IV. ASSARAH B'TEVETH ("Tenth of Teveth" — Tenth Month).

On this day began the siege of Jerusalem by Nebuchadnezzar. Now in Israel this fast is observed also as a Memorial Day for the six million Jews who were massacred by the Nazis in the second World War (1939-1945).

V. TAANITH ESTHER ("Fast of Esther") falls on the day before the day of PURIM. It commemorates the fasting of Esther and the praying of the people that God might frustrate Haman's design to exterminate the Jewish people (see "Purim"). (Also, see Esther 4:16.)

There was a *sixth fast,* but this is to be kept only by first-born males. It falls on the day preceding Passover, in memory of the death of the first-born of Egypt, before the exodus, while the Jewish first-born were spared.

Pious Jews observed various other fasts, either self-inflicted as penitence, or fixed ones on various occasions, which the people as a whole are not enjoined to keep.

On all the fast days there are certain variations of the daily prayers. With the exception of TISHAH B'AV, all the minor fasts begin at daybreak and last until nightfall. (Tishah B'av, like Yom Kippur, begins with the previous evening.)

When a fast day falls on a Sabbath it is transferred to a week-day.

Isaiah, who in the first chapter tells of the *New Moon* and the Sabbath, as well as the other holydays, and the sacrifices and that they have become an abomination unto God, concludes his last chapter with the reassuring, reconciling words: "And it shall come to pass that from one New Moon to another, and from one Sabbath to another, shall *all flesh* come to worship before me, saith the Lord" (Isaiah 66:23).

CHAPTER VIII

THE LAWS AND CUSTOMS OF THE JEWISH PEOPLE

The KITZUR SHULCHAN ARUCH (Condensed Code of Laws), the popular guide to Jewish living, starts out with the motto: "I have set the Lord always before me" (Psalm 16:8), and goes on saying that the consiousness of God's omnipresence will assuredly keep the Jew from sin and indecency. It says that a man standing before a king will be very careful that his every action, every movement, every word be pleasing to his Majesty.

Thus, with this precept in mind, the life of the religious Jew is governed in all its phases, during all his waking hours. As soon as he awakens from his night's sleep he recites: "I thank Thee, O eternal King, because Thou hast graciously restored my soul to me, great is Thy faithfulness." Then begins his service of God, not only by the daily prayers, in the morning and evening, and the various benedictions prescribed for the various sorts of food, and the various experiences, but also, almost every action of his, is to be performed punctiliously in accord with the tradition: What to wear, and how to dress; how to wash, when to wash; what to eat, when to eat and how to eat. Even his private natural needs, he is to satisfy according to prescription. And most of his actions, whether of profane or sacred nature, are preceded and followed by a set of benedictions or some pious formula. This religious life, as if always aware of the presence of the King-Creator, is to go on incessantly during all conscious life — "from the cradle to the grave."

Some of the Jewish customs and usages are based on some biblical precepts, and others came into Jewish life by certain historical experiences, and these, too, have been sanctioned by some passage, or word, in the Bible, which the rabbis have cleverly adapted. But some usages of doubtful origin, even if infiltrated from heathen sources, have been sanctioned by long years of practice. The popular saying is: "A custom breaks the law" — meaning that the observance of the custom nullifies the law (which it breaks) and is, thus, to be preferred. The custom is given the prerogative.

Present-day Jewry which is in a state of religious transition and perplexity has become skeptical about the traditions of the rabbis and fathers, including some old hallowed usages. Yet most of the people still cling to certain laws and customs purely from sentimental motives. To these belong the rites or ceremonies of Circumcision, Bar-Mitzvah, Marriage, Mourning, Lighting of Sabbath Candles, *Kosher*, the "Seder" on the Eve of Passover and some others. Of all these only circumcision is built on and about the solid rock of divine command.

We shall try to acquaint our readers with the most important usages which are still generally observed, although less rigidly and with some minor variations by various groups.

CIRCUMCISION

The oldest and most sacred of Jewish rites is circumcision (*Milah*). It is the removal of the foreskin of the male organ by means of cutting. It is called *brith* or *brith milah*, or *brith Abraham*, i.e. the Abrahamic Covenant (see Genesis 17:9-14, and Leviticus 12:3). This rite has been preserved most faithfully all through the ages.

Originally every father actually circumcised his child, but in course of time every Jewish Community had a professional operator Mohel — Circumciser. This rite which is performed on the eighth day after the child's birth is accompanied with various impressive ceremonies.

We wonder whether some of these ceremonies and recitations were not introduced by the early Christians who still circumcised their children at the synagogue. Many of these rites are symbolic of the Messiah and the New Covenant as recorded in the New Testament. When the child is brought in for circumcision the congregations call out: "Blessed be he who comes in the name of God." Then the child is placed on a chair which is called the "Throne of Elijah." Elijah, according to the rabbis, is the "Angel of the Covenant" of Malachi 3:23. The "Mohel" recites a prayer which begins: "This is the throne of Elijah . . . For Thy salvation, O Lord, I have waited. . . ."

Then comes the recitation and benediction over a goblet of wine. The God-father (*Sandak*) drinks of the wine, inserts a few drops of it into the mouth of the infant, and the remainder is sent to the mother. It is at this rite when the infant is given a Hebrew name, which will henceforth be used as legal or ritual name although it may be supplemented by an additional non-Hebrew name.

At the conclusion of the rite a prayer is recited wherein are the following significant lines: "May the All-merciful, regardful of the merit of them that are akin by the blood of the circumcision, send us *His Messiah*, .walking in His integrity, to bring good tidings and consolation to the people that is scattered and dispersed among the Peoples. . . . May the All-merciful, send us the Righteous Priest who remains withdrawn in concealment, until a throne, bright as the sun and the diamond, shall be prepared for Him, the prophet who covered His face with His mantle and wrapped Himself therein, with whom our covenant was made in life and peace. . . . May the All-merciful make us worthy of the days of the Messiah, and of the life of the world to come." Here the Messiah, the Righteous Priest, (even the Angel of the Covenant), is one and the same person — as Jesus was understood to be, by His early Jewish followers, and which modern Jews fail to recognize, although they have been reciting these and other "Christian" prayers and observing "Christian" rites, as on Passover Eve, for centuries.

Circumcision ceremonies usually conclude with a feast at home or with some "treat" of liquor and cake to the congregation after the morning service.

Girls receive their names about six weeks after their birth, on a Sabbath day, when the father is called to the Bemah in the synagogue (to be one of the eight persons) to recite the usual benedictions over a subsection of the weekly portion read from the scroll of the Torah. Then the father requests the precentor, or the "Gabbai," to dedicate a special blessing to his new daughter who is now called by the name the father chooses for her. Whereupon the congregation responds with: *"Mazaltov"* ("Good Luck").

(No ceremonies, no feasts follow the birth of a female child.)

Many of the old customs that had been observed about child birth, especially during the first week after birth, have lately fallen into disuse because the people became aware of their superstitious nature.

PIDYON HABEN
(Redemption of the First Born Son)

According to the Bible (Exodus 13:2, 12-15, and Numbers 18:13-16), the first born male child must be redeemed on the thirty-first day of his birth. Exempt from this duty is the father who is a Kohen[1] or a Levi, or if the mother is the daughter of a Kohen or Levi.

If the thirty-first day falls on a Sabbath or holiday the ceremony is postponed to the following day. The main feature of this rite of Redemption is the father's presenting his child (usually on a silver tray) to the Kohen declaring his wish to redeem him for five shekels in accordance with God's commandment. (The equivalent of five shekels in our currency is about $2.50.)

After the Kohen has received the redemption money he returns the child to the father, whereupon the father recites certain set benedictions. Then the Kohen holding the money over the head of the child recites: *"This is instead of that, this in commutation of that, this in remission of that. May this child enter into life, into the Law and the fear of Heaven. May it be God's Will that even as he has been admitted to redemption, so may he enter into the Law, the nuptial canopy, and into good deeds. Amen."* Then he places his hand over the head of the child and pronounces a blessing which contains also the priestly blessing: *"The Lord bless thee and keep thee, the Lord make His face to shine upon thee, and be gracious unto thee, and give thee peace."* After the redemption there is a feast similar to the one following the ceremony of circumcision. Unlike circumcision which all Jews observe, "Redemption of the Son" is falling into disuse.

Bar Mitzvah
(Literally: "Son of Commandment" — "Man of Duty")

One of the most favorite customs and practices is the "Bar Mitzvah" celebration. As the circumcision rite brings the male child into the "Covenant of Abraham," thus making him a Jew, so the Bar Mitzvah rites, when he reaches the age of thirteen years, make him a religious, a responsible Jew. He then becomes a full-fledged member of the Jewish community sharing with it all duties and privileges. On the first Sabbath of his fourteenth year, at the morning service in the synagogue, he is called up to read a part of the weekly portion of the Torah and the weekly portion of the prophets ("Haftarah"). These are preceded and concluded by his reciting certain benedictions. The father who stands by calls out, "Blessed be He who has relieved (freed) me from the responsibility of this child's doing." From that time on

[1] See "Vocabulary."

the boy has attained ritual maturity. He may now be one of a *Minyan* (a ten men quorum needed for "congregation" service). He may then lead the congregation in prayer, read the Torah and perform all religious duties which a mature Jew may perform. The ceremony at the synagogue is usually followed by festivities at home when the boy gives an address on some biblical or Talmudic theme, and gladly inspects the presents his friends and relatives have brought him.

Like most of the Jewish customs the Bar Mitzvah, too, has no biblical basis and there is no indication in the Talmudic writings that there existed such a practice. Its existence as a Jewish custom cannot be traced back further than the fourteenth century. There is no doubt that the "Bar Mitzvah" came into being as a Jewish religious institution, as a result of Christian influences and corresponds to the rite of Confirmation in the church. (See Dembitz, *Services in Synagogue and Home*, p. 263, and *Jewish Life in the Middle Ages*, p. 32).

Christian confirmation rites have had still more influence on the "liberal" or "Reform" Jews, who include also girls in the rites of confirmation. A girl celebrating such ceremonies is called *Bath-Mitzvah* (i.e. "Daughter of Commandment"). This innovation is not in harmony with rabbinic law which does not expect women to perform religious obligations, and thus girls are not to be subjected to "Mitzvah" ceremonies. There are only three Affirmative Commandments which Jewish women are expected to observe. They are *Challah*,[2] *Niddah* and the *Kindling of the Sabbath Candles*.

But (we may say) liberal Judaism does not have to differentiate between male and female Jews, because neither is expected to keep the various ritual laws, and both sexes ignore them alike.

MARRIAGE

The age of marriage among Jews is usually the same as among their non-Jewish neighbors, although the Jewish code, "Shulchan Aruch," states: "Every Jewish man should marry at eighteen, and he who marries earlier is more meritorious. No one, however, should marry earlier than thirteen years of age." The restrictions in selecting a spouse on account of affinity, chastity, religion are about the same as are among Christians, excepting that a *Kohen* (Aaronite, or priestly descent) may not marry

[2] See "Vocabulary."

a divorced woman (see Leviticus 21:6, 7, 14). During the Middle Ages, up to modern times, marriages have been arranged by professional marriage brokers (match-makers — *Shadchan*). This profession is not altogether extinct. Even here in America, many a Jewish marriage was made possible by the "Shadchan," although it may have a more modern name.

The nuptial ceremony is performed by a rabbi, under a canopy *(chuppah)*, made of silk or satin, supported by four staves (one on each corner) and held by the guests (4). Sometimes a *tallith* (a praying shawl) is used instead of the silk covering. The act of marriage is called *kiddushin* (sanctification). The main ceremony is the groom's placing a ring, without stone, upon the forefinger of the right hand of the bride and saying: "*Thou art sanctified (consecrated) unto me by this ring according to the law of Moses and Israel.*" The consecration by ring originated in medieval times, as a substitute for the coin by which marriages were originally consummated. The groom then places a glass on the ground and breaks it with his foot, after which the guests shout joyfully, "*Mazal tov — mazal tov,*" good luck, good luck. The breaking of the glass is doubtless of some ancient pagan origin. It is interpreted as a reminder of the destruction of the temple and Jerusalem.

This ceremony is preceded by various recitations and benedictions. One of the benedictions which the officiating rabbi recites over a cup of wine, ends with: ". . . Blessed art thou, O Lord, who sanctifiest thy people Israel by the (rite of the) canopy and the covenant of wedlock." Both groom and bride drink some drops of this wine. Much time of the ceremony is occupied by the reading of the "Kethubah" or marriage contract, wherein the cu - tomary obligations of married life are specified, and in particular the settlement on the wife of a certain amount payable at her husband's death or on her being divorced. The "Kethubah" is retained by the wife. This contract is written in Aramaic — the language of the Talmud and the Targums.

Bride and groom are expected to fast on the day of their marriage as a mark of their penitence for sins they committed up to that day, so that they may start together a God-fearing, pious life.

After the ceremony, which is usually conducted at the synagogue, a feast is held at home accompanied by set prayers and singing of customary songs — usually of a religious nature.

THE "GET"
(Bill of Divorce)

The Jewish divorce laws are based on the Mosaic Law ("When a man hath taken a wife, and married her, and it come to pass that she find no favour in his eyes, because he hath found some uncleanness in her: then let him write her a bill of divorcement, and give it in her hand, and send her out of his house. And when she is departed out of his house, she may go and be another man's wife" — Deuteronomy 24:1, 2). According to this passage the right of divorce was granted to the husband with no provision of the same right to the wife. But the *Kethubah* (marriage contract) which stipulates a dowry in case of divorce tends to prevent the abuse of the husband's privilege. Today the Jewish divorce laws are about the same as are customary in the Western world. The later rabbinic laws governing divorce have, undoubtedly, been influenced by the principles expressed in the New Testament about the equality of rights of man and woman, husband and wife.

Like the *Kethubah*, the *Get*, too, is written in Aramaic, but the *Get* is handwritten on parchment, as are the passages in the *Mezuzzah* and in *Tephillin*, as well as are the Scrolls of the Torah. The *Get* is always conducted in the presence of a *Minyan*, a religious quorum of ten men. The main features of the bill are the place, the date, the names of the parties, the signatures of the witnesses, and the phrases which express separation in unequivocal terms.

CHALITZAH
("Drawing Off")

According to Leviticus 18:16; 20:21, and Deuteronomy 25:5-10, a brother of the man who died leaving a widow but no children, is obliged to marry this widow. This is known as "Levirate marriage," or in Hebrew: *"Yibum."* If the brother refuses to marry the widow, she is to report the matter to the Rabbinate, which then calls the brother and in the presence of three judges, usually the Rabbi and chief officers of the congregation, the *Chalitzah* ceremony is performed.

The important feature of this ceremony is: The widow "draws off" the shoe of her brother-in-law, whereupon she spits into his face and calls out: "So shall it be done to the man that will not build up his brother's house."

In course of time the practice of Levirate marriage has become objectionable especially in Christian countries where polygamy was outlawed (by a decree of Rabbi Gershom Ben Judah, 960-1028),[3] so that only *Chalitzah* has to be performed to release the widow's brother-in-law of his obligation to marry her.

SOME OF THE RITES AND CEREMONIES (CUSTOMS) IN JEWISH LIFE CONCERNING DEATH

On hearing of the death of a relative the Jew is to recite "God has given, God has taken, Blessed be the Truthful Judge."

At the death of a near relative, the rite of *K'ria'ah*, Rending of Garment, is performed as an outward sign of grief. Usually after the coffin is lowered into the grave, a cut, or tear, is made at the lapel of the outer garment. If for some reason the relative was not then at the cemetery, he is to rend the garment as soon as he hears of the death.

The *Chevrah Kadishah* (Holy Association) is an organization which every Jewish community has to care for the funeral rites. Their members are at the death-bed to recite with the dying person the *vidui* (confession), and after the death occurs they cleanse the corpse (*taharah*) and shroud it (in *tachrichin*) and accompany it (*l'vayah*) to the cemetery where they bury it with the customary rites. Every Jew in the neighborhood feels it his duty to accompany the funeral procession, at least a part of the way, to "extend to the deceased last honor." During the procession, collectors of free will offering go about chanting: "Charity saves from death" (Proverbs 10:2; 11:9).

Jews of priestly descent (*kohen*) are not allowed to come near the dead, nor enter the cemetery.

In the belief that the resurrection will take place only in the Holy Land, some Jews place some earth brought from Palestine under the body in the coffin.

The dead are usually buried shrouded in plain white linen, and in a plain board coffin. This simple attire and coffin is to emphasize the equality of all men in death (See Job 1:21).

The *Kaddish*, an old prayer, written in the Aramaic language, sanctifying the name of God, was adapted during the late Middle Ages (for some reason) as a prayer for the dead. The recitation of the *Kaddish* by the mourners at the services in the synagogue has, according to the rabbis, the efficacy of redeeming

[3] Oriental Jews, in opposition to Ashkenazi Jews, don't feel themselves obliged to practice monogamy and thus as their non-Christian neighbors may marry more than one wife.

or, at least allaying the dead from suffering in Gehenom.[4] It is recited by the mourners at the grave, and all through the mourning year (the eleven months after the departure) at the daily services. Then it is repeated on every anniversary of the death — the so-called *Yarzeit*. During *Yarzeit as well as during Shiva'a* a "soul-candle" is to burn at home, all night and day.

Mourning. The first seven days (*Shiva'a*) the mourner is confined to his home, where he is to sit on the floor. Since he may not leave his home, Jewish neighbors, friends or passersby come in to form a *Minyan* for the daily services. During the *Shiva'a* the mourner may not perform any manual labor or business transactions. During the "Seven Days" he is not permitted to wear shoes, to cut his hair, or shave or take a bath, nor anything that may afford him pleasure, not even to study sacred books, except those that arouse sadness and grief, as the book of Job and similar writings. During these days people come in to console him.

The usual formula of Consolation is, or starts with, "May God comfort you with all those who mourn for Zion and Jerusalem."

Certain restrictions of mourning are continued through the first month (*Shlosim* — 30 days of mourning), and some restrictions go on for the whole of the first year (keep away from music and all forms of entertainment).

Another occasion of hallowing the memory of the dead, is the so-called *Yizkor* ("May He remember"), or *Mazkir Neshamoth* — a memorial service conducted during the public service in the synagogue on *Yom Kippur,* and on the last day of Pesach and Succoth. Many Jews, especially women, even such as do not usually attend synagogue, are present at this Memorial Prayer. There are set prayers for various relatives. For the father, for instance, the prayer is: "May God remember the soul of our honored father (here comes his name and the name of the father's father) who is gone to his repose, for that, I now solemnly offer charity for his sake; in reward of this, may his soul enjoy eternal life, with the souls of Abraham, Isaac, and Jacob; Sarah, Rebecca, Rachel and Leah, and the rest of the righteous males and females that are in Paradise; and let us say, Amen."

Non-mourners leave the room while these prayers are recited and return when they are over. It is believed that the departed souls (of the near kin) are present in the synagogue at that prayer. Non-relatives might be harmed if present.

---

[4] See "Vocabulary."

Those of the less-observant mourners, especially women, leave the synagogue soon after *Yizkor.*

(There is heart-rending weeping and sobbing during this prayer).

KOSHER

Kosher, means "fit," "suitable." In Jewish lore it refers to food which is ritually fit to be eaten. When food is not *kosher* it is *treif* or *treifa,* signifying "unfit" (taboo) for Jewish consumption. The laws governing the ritual fitness of food are called *Kashruth.*

Now this *Kashruth,* it may truly be said, is the center and circumference of modern observant Judaism. It occupies the greatest part of Jewish home life and practices, and it provides the greatest part of the income of the Jewish hierarchy. Rabbis, Ritual Slaughterers, Kosher butchers, various supervisors (inspectors) make their livelihood by maintaining these laws. These laws, which are "innumerable," have no real biblical foundation. Moses, the Jewish lawgiver, as codified in the Pentateuch, if he were to look at Kashruth would not be able to understand or recognize any of them as "Jewish."

All this multitude of peculiar practices is built around the Scriptural commandment: "Thou shalt not boil a kid in its mother's milk" (Exodus 23:19; 34:26, and repeated again in Deuteronomy 14:21). The rabbis have made this kid stand for all kinds of meat-products, and its mother's milk for all dairy products, and nothing that comes from meat could be mixed with anything that comes from milk. The strict separation between the two involves not only separate utensils, as pots and pans, plates, knives, spoons, etc., but also washbasins, tablecloths and napkins. The extremely pious even have separate sculleries and ranges.

Thus every Jewish household has three sets of vessels; one set for meats and meat products, one for milk and milk products, and a third for neutral foods as fruit, vegetables and also fish. Besides these three sets, there are three separate sets for the Passover when nothing that had been used for or had touched unleaven bread could be used during the eight days of Passover.

After a Jew eats meat he is to wait at least six hours before he may eat any milk products, because, as the rabbis have figured out, it takes six hours before meat is digested, so if some milky food reaches the stomach before the meat is fully digested they may unlawfully mix there. Milk is supposed to digest within half an hour, so meat may be eaten half an hour after milk has been consumed.

Meat is considered as *Kosher*, not just if it comes from a Kosher animal according to Mosaic Law (Leviticus XI), but has also been killed ritually by a specially qualified *Shochet* (Slaughterer), and then passed scrupulous scrutiny of the flesh, to see if the animal was not diseased. Then certain "unclean" parts must be removed before the meat is pronounced as Kosher. The Kosher inspector then affixes a seal indicating its fitness. But even then there are certain rigid requirements to be fulfilled to make the meat fit to be eaten. Every drop of blood is to be extracted from it. This is done by first soaking it in water for a certain specified time, then salt is sprinkled on it and so it is to stand for a specified time; then it is carefully rinsed and placed on a draining board or grate till it is thoroughly drained. Then only is it ready for cooking, and as said previously, in specially "meaty" ("fleishig") vessels. If some dairy products, or a utensil (let us say — a spoon) once used for dairy products happens to come in contact with the meat, then the meat as well as the vessels containing it are "treif" and ritually unfit for use.

The Kosher laws involve also various other practices and inhibitions; for example, bread is considered as Kosher only after a part of the dough from which it is made has been separated and ritually burned (see *Challah*). Another example: wine that a Gentile had touched is no longer Kosher.

Strict observance of *Kashruth* becomes rarer day by day. Yet this is still considered as the most important part of what is called Judaism. The other important part of Judaism is the heap of Sabbath laws, which, too, have only a faint basis in Scriptural Judaism, and which, too, are rapidly falling into disuse.

Take away these man-made food laws and Sabbath laws from "Judaism," and next to nothing is left of rabbinic Judaism.

Miscellaneous

There are also innumerable customs connected with the various feasts and fast days, and occasions of various private or family events. Mention may be made here that special articles of food are being prepared for each holiday, as well as special food being provided for the Sabbath (*Chulent, Kugel, Gefillte fish*). (On Pesach — Kneidlach, matze-braten, and on Purim, Haman Tashen, etc.)

Another peculiar custom may be mentioned: The perpetual covering of the head. While the Jewish married woman must have her head covered for the sake of decency, the man, too, must cover his head for some unknown reason. This custom is not mentioned in ancient Jewish literature. The Bible speaks of a head cover only for the priest as part of his official garb.

Yet the orthodox Jew considers bareheadedness as a serious breach of Judaism, so he is careful to have on a small skull cap, a "*cappel*" or "*yarmulka*," when for some reason he has to take off his larger head-dress. With modern orthodox Jews the *yarmulka* has become the only outward sign and symbol of Judaism. Old-fashioned Jews still cling to their typically "Jewish" garb besides their untrimmed beard and sidelocks *(peoth)* which distinguish them as Jews, different than *goyim* (Gentiles).

CHAPTER IX

JEWISH LITERATURE

The Jewish people have often been referred to as "The People of the Book." The "book" probably originally meant the "Bible." But one might as well say, "the people of books." Not only has this people produced more literature than any other people in the world, comparatively speaking, but also there is or was no other people that had so much reverence, respect and love for books, for their authors, and for those who are learned and well-versed in books. The hero in Jewish life, legend and genealogy has never been, as with the Gentiles, one of brawn, but of brain. The *talmid chacham* — the "wise scholar" — was the ideal type in Jewish estimation. The *am ha' aretz,* the ignorant, has always been the subject of contempt.

For the last 2,000 years and perhaps centuries earlier, there were hardly any illiterate male Jews. Every Jewish *boy* attended some kind of school. Schooling usually began when the boy was only three years old. At the age of five he was already initiated in the study of the Pentateuch in the original Hebrew and translated into the vernacular. At thirteen when he became *bar mitzvah,* "a son of the law," a full-fledged member of the community, he could deliver an oration on an intricate Talmudical subject full of hair-splitting casuistry ("pilpul"). If after some more years of schooling he distinguished himself as a "talmid chachan," he was, as a rule, "snatched" up as a son-in-law by well-to-do parents, in whose house he could continue his studies for several more years.

His studies were, almost entirely, in the Talmudic books and their commentaries and in books of later dates, dealing with Jewish laws.

On rare occasions he may have glanced into the Bible, besides the Pentateuch, in which almost every Jew was well-versed.

Besides the large libraries (of "sacred books") which every community possessed and usually kept in the synagogues, open and free to all at all times, every Jewish home had a library of its own, each according to its means. Cases or shelves well-stocked with books were considered as the best ornaments of the Jewish home.

Even the poorest, ignorant family had at least its own liturgical books, such as a *siddur* ("order," meaning order of service), which contained the daily prayers and benedictions for various occasions; a *machzor* — series of prayer books for each of the various holy days; *Selichot* (Supplications), a book containing the prayers which are recited in the early mornings (or late at nights) several days before New Year and between New Year and the Day of Atonement; *Kinnoth* — a book of elegies and prayers, containing also the "Book of Lamentations," which is recited on the fast of the Ninth of Av (the memorial day of the destruction of the Temples); *Haggada* ("Legend") containing the "prayers," etc., which are recited and chanted on the Eve of Passover (Seder); *Megillah* — (Scroll) — meaning the "Book of Esther" which is read both on the Eve and the Day of Purim; *Thillim* — The Psalter, which has always been a handy book and steady companion, to be read on various occasions, in time of illness, of danger, of worry, or just for pleasure in spare time; *Chumash* — meaning the "five" books of Moses. This book is divided into weekly portions, which are read in the synagogues during the morning service of the Sabbath, each Sabbath a different portion, so that during the year the whole book is publicly recited (read). The same portion was also read privately at home, and it usually was studied during that week in "Cheder" (elementary school).

All these books were necessary for the "divine service" at the synagogue or at home. As to commentaries for study of the "Torah," their number and variety depended on the state of learning of the male members of the family.

While the women were not obliged to pray or attend services at the synagogue, they often did pray at home. On Sabbaths and festivals when they attended the synagogue, they used either the same books as the males, or the same books together with a translation in the vernacular (in Yiddish). In European communities the Jewish women also had some books in Yiddish of their own, such as the *Deutsh-Chumash*, a free translation of the Chumash richly mixed with expositions and legends from the Talmudic books. Another favorite book was *T'chinoth* (supplications), prayers in Yiddish for various occasions, and there were other books specifically prepared for women in Yiddish.

Within the limits of this discussion it is possible to give only the briefest of brief accounts of the Hebrew literature which began some three millennia ago. The Bible, the "Book of Books," mentions various books which disappeared during the ages. As early as the time of Moses, someone wrote a book called "Book of the Wars of the Lord" — (see Numbers 21:14). It must have been quite popular at that time.

Ecclesiastes (12:12) warns against the many and innumerable books. The recent discoveries of scrolls at the Dead Sea reveal that the Jews had about the time of Christ many books besides the Bible and the Apocrypha.

After the destruction of the second Commonwealth and the dispersion of the Jewish people, their literary production received a serious setback. For long years the rabbis outlawed all books besides the Bible. The Bible was called *Torah She'bichtav* (written Torah) in distinction to the *Torah She-balpeh* (oral Torah), which were laws and customs that became part of Jewish life during the centuries after Moses. According to the Rabbis these laws were already handed down from Sinai, but for certain reasons were not then incorporated in the written law. They were to be delivered orally from generation to generation. However, since there was the danger that in exile these oral laws might be forgotten, the rabbis decided to write them down. The result of that decision was *The Talmud* — a monumental work which was about 500 years in the making. It is not strictly a code of laws, although it contains all the laws which were enacted up to the time of its completion, but also contains exposition and interpretations of the "Written Law," as well as some historical events and legends and much superstition mixed with scientific facts.

Side by side with the Talmud there came into being the *Midrash* (or in the plural, *Midrashim*, books dealing with the homiletic exposition of the Bible, mainly of the Pentateuch). These, like the Haggadah part of the Talmud, became very popular with the Jewish masses, since they were written in Hebrew, in the moving, narrative style, not like the *Halachah*, which was mostly in Aramaic, intricate and less appealing to the heart, even to the legalistic heart of the Jew. (See chapter on "Talmud and Midrash.")

The *Targums* (Translations) form a set of books which usually come under the heading of Exegesis. (See chapter on "Exegesis.")

The Kabbalist Books: These are the mystical interpretation of the Scriptures. Sometime around 1200 A.D. there arose in Spain a tendency and belief that the Bible, or religion as a whole, might best be understood by faith and spiritual insight and contemplation rather than by the ordinary sense perception or the use of logical reasoning. (See chapter on "The Kabbalah.")

The Kabbalah had a profound influence on the pseudo-Messianic movement of *Shabathai Zvi*, and later upon the Chassidic movement which arose in Poland in the eighteenth century.

The Chassidic movements have produced a large number of books, some homiletic, but mostly narrative, biographies of certain wonder-rabbis. These books were very popular at their inception, but are now seldom read.

Among the most famous post-Talmudic books which profoundly inspired Judaism (with an enduring effect) are:

Emunoth We-deoth (Dogmas and Truths) by Saadya Gaon (892-942).

Chovath Halvavoth (Duties of the Hearts) by Bachya ben Joseph in the eleventh century. This is the first Jewish system of ethics. In it, the writer insists on the need of fulfilling the spirit of the Law rather than its letter.

Moreh Nevochim (Guide of the Perplexed) by Rabbi Moses ben Maimon (1135-1204) or as he is known by the initials of his name "RaMBaM." To the Gentiles he is known as Maimonides. Most of his books became classics in Jewish literature. In his time he was regarded with disfavor by many of the leading rabbis, mainly because of his heretical teaching as expressed in his book, *Moreh Nevochim*, which was considered dangerous to rabbinic orthodoxy. Later he was regarded as the greatest Jewish genius since the first Moses.

While in his other books he showed himself to be a faithful disciple of the rabbis of old, in this book he ran counter to rabbinic teaching. In it he attempts to show that Judaism is the very expression of human intelligence, that there is nothing in Judaism, if properly explained, which contradicts true philosophy. Thus he sought to spiritualize what seemed to be "contradictory to true philosophy," and interpret it in the allegorical manner of the Alexanderines (Philo, etc.). And yet, paradoxically, this man, who in his time was suspected of heresy and even atheism, became the author of the so-called Jewish Creed or Confession of faith. In his commentary on the Mishnah he enunciates thirteen principles of the faith which every Jew ought to believe. These principles (in Hebrew, *Ikkarim*) were generally accepted and embodied in the Prayer Book and are to be recited daily, except on Sabbath and holydays.

The "Moreh Nevochim" was generally outlawed by the Rabbis, especially was it forbidden to the younger students who might be misled into unbelief, and yet it was published again and again, and was studied, often secretly, by young and old.

Kuzari by Yehuda Helevi (1085-1140). This author is generally regarded as the greatest of Hebrew poets, many of whose poems are embodied in the Jewish liturgy. The Kuzari was first written for the benefit of the ruler of the Kuzarim (Khazars). It is in the form of "Apologia" and justifies Judaism as against Philosophy, Christianity and Mohammedanism. The Khazars were then converted to Judaism.

The books that exercised the most powerful influence on (later) Judaism, however, were the various codes.

CODIFICATION

The Talmud, although it contained, as it was intended to, all the Rabbinic Law, could not for long serve its purpose. It was too lengthy, difficult and confusing for the average Jew, and it became necessary to make shorter cómpendiums and codifications, omitting all the non-legal portions (stories, etc.) and the legal discussions.

Among the systematic codes are the *Rif* or *Alfasi* (in the eleventh century).

The *Mishneh Torah* (Repetition of the Law) by the "Rambam," consists of fourteen volumes, sometimes called *Yad Hachazakah,* and is written in Hebrew so that anyone knowing this language could easily read it (1180 A.D.).

The *Turim*, a four volume book: 1. Dealing with liturgical laws; 2. Ritual laws; 3. Marriage laws; 4. Civil laws. This code is the more practical as it restricts itself to the laws actually in use at the time. It omits all laws that had become obsolete, and embodies all laws and customs that came into practice after the completion of the Talmud.

The *Shulchan Aruch* — this is the most extensively used of the various Codifications. It was written by Joseph Karo in the sixteenth century and has become the guiding authority on Jewish practice. It is this code that the Jews have since been consulting to learn *what is the law* (what to do and what not to do).

Kitzur Shulchan Aruch (Abridged Shulchan Aruch), written in simple language, contains only those laws and customs which are generally practiced. It disregards the laws that are only occasionally used. When such an occasion arises, a Rabbi has to be consulted. This abridged compendium was widely spread.

Besides the various codes there are also The Responsa books, compilations of questions and replies. Whenever some legal question arose which was not mentioned in the extant codes, it was put before one of the great authorities of the age. Such questions and the authoritative reply to them were recorded for reference.

There were also several books, mostly poetic, of a religious nature, many of which were incorporated in Jewish liturgy for various occasions.

Since the *Haskalah* (Enlightenment) movement the Jewish people have produced a vast literature which is mainly secular. Most of the books were written in Hebrew, a great many in Yiddish, and others in the various languages of the countries where large Jewish communities lived.

Among the great authors of secular books: novels, poems, etc. are: Mendele Mocher S'farim, Perez, Shalom Aleichem, Shalom Ash, Bialik, and Chernichovski.

CHAPTER X

EXEGESIS OF THE BIBLE

After the Jews had produced the Bible, they started to explain it, and they have been doing this explaining ever since. Most of the innumerable books the Jews have produced during the last 22 centuries are concerned with explaining, elucidating, interpreting and expounding the Bible. The books of the Talmud, the Targums, the various *Midrashim,* the philosophic Philo to Maimonides, and others, are all in one way or another commentaries on the Bible.

Since the Jew has to live by the "Law of God," every word, every iota of the Holy Scriptures was to serve as a sign post to direct his way in the complexities of life. Thus every word had to be unmistakably clear and well defined.

First came the Targum (Translation).

THE TARGUMS AND EXEGESIS

For many centuries following the Babylonian exile the Jewish language was Aramaic. The Bible which, with some exceptions, was in Hebrew, was no longer well understood by the masses. It was thus necessary to translate it into the vernacular and to explain difficult passages. Thus, on the Sabbath and Holy Days when a portion of the Hebrew Bible was read in the synagogue, one of the learned men — the Rabbi or an official translator ("Meturgeman") — translated the Hebrew text into Aramaic and when necessary also often expounded it. In countries where the Jews spoke Greek, they used the Septuagint, a translation made about 270 B.C., by *seventy* emissaries from Jerusalem for Ptolemy II, then king of Egypt. In Hebrew it is known as *Targum Hashiv'im,* translation of the seventy, which is also the meaning of *septuaginta* (in Greek).

With the exception of this early translation which was written down, the Aramaic Targums were oral, like the "Oral Law." It was after the destruction of Jerusalem and the second exile that the Aramaic Targums were written down. The best known Targum is that called *Onkelos* to the Pentateuch, and it is on the whole a literal translation. The other Targums are generally paraphrastic. Such is the *Targum Yerushalmi* (The Jerusalem translation and Targum Jonathan).[1] Onkelos, whose translation bears his name, is said to have been a pupil of Rabbi Gamaliel and may have known Paul at the same school. The Targum Yerushalmi in its present form was written not earlier than the seventh century A.D.

The Targums shed much light on ancient Jewish Theology and exegesis, and often show that there was no difference between the New Testament interpretation and the rabbinic interpretation of certain Messianic passages in the Old Testament. It is only much later, in the Middle Ages, that the Rabbis found it necessary to interpret certain passages differently.

There is a marked tendency in the Targums to avoid anthropomorphisms. For example, for "the Lord came down" (Genesis 11:25) the Targum has, "the Lord revealed Himself." The transcendence of God is emphasized by the employment of intermediate agencies like the *Memra* (the "Word" or the "Logos" — in Greek — as used by John: "In the beginning was the Word"), the "Shekinah," etc. Or another example: Genesis 3:8 the Targum translates: "And they heard the voice of the *Memra* of God walking in the garden . . ." (We shall return to this subject in a later chapter dealing with the Trinity.)

The Targums have served not only as a translation of the Scriptures but also as an explanation and exposition. When, however, there arose large Jewish communities in Europe, where Aramaic was no longer the Jewish vernacular, there had to be new commentaries on the Scriptures.

The greatest of the Commentators was *Rashi*, Rabbi Shlomo Itzchaki, famous also as the commentator of the Talmud, who lived in France (1040-1105). The commentary is usually printed below the Hebrew text. Jewish children began the study of *"Chumash with Rashi"* at an early age and this is still customary in the schools of Israel and is widely used in most Jewish schools in diaspora.

---

[1] There are no sure data as to the authorship of the various Targums, nor as to the time of their authorship. It is surmised that "Onkelos" was written in the second century A.D.;"Jonathan" (to the Prophets) in the fourth century; "Yerushalmi" (or pseudo Jonathan) in the seventh century, and the others even later.

Among the other notable exegetes of the Middle Ages whose works have been accepted as authoritative and sacred are:

SAADIA, Rabbenu Saadiah Gaon, born 892 in Egypt, died 942 in Babylon. A most revered Rabbi whose books have left an indelible impression upon Judaism.

RAMBAM (MAIMONIDES), is considered as a great commentator of the Bible, although his book, *More Nevochim*, was usually shunned because of its non-Jewish spirit. Yet, because of his other voluminous books which are strictly in the rabbinic spirit, he was often called "Second Moses." Indeed, since Moses, son of Amram, no other Jew has wielded such an influence upon Judaism as has Moses, son of Maimon — known as "RMBM."

IBN EZRA (Abraham), born 1093 in Spain, died 1167 in Rome; a Hebrew poet and one of the greatest Bible exegetes.

KIMCHI, or R'D'K (Rabbi David Kimchi), lived in France 1160-1235. Philolog and commentator.

RAMBAN — (Rabbi Moshe ben Nachman), known also as Nachmanides, born in Spain 1194, died in Palestine in 1270. Revered as a great Rabbi and commentator of great renown.

RABBI BACHYA — ben Asher of Spain (in thirteenth century). His commentary on the five books of Moses became one of the most popular exegetical works.

RaLBaG (initials of Rabbi Levi ben Gershon) died in 1344, recognized as one of the great exegetes.

ABARBANEL (Rabbi Isaac Abravanel), born in Lisbon, Portugal, 1437, died in Venice, Italy, in 1508. He was one of the most famous authorities on Judaism, and one of the greatest exegetes.

RABBI MOSES ALSHECH of Palestine in sixteenth century, was the most prolific exegetical author on most of the Bible.

YARCHI in the twelfth century in France was another of the recognized great exegetes.

THE PESIKTA, PIRKE D'RABBI ELIEZER, and the YALKUT of the thirteenth century are Haggadic compilations and have been considered as sacred as the older Midrashim.

The ZOHAR on the Pentateuch (see KABBALAH) explains the Bible in the mystic way of the Kabbalah. This book has been kept by observant Jews, especially by the Chassidim, as very sacred, and is referred to as the *Holy Zohar*.

According to the expositors of the Bible, and of Judaism as a whole, the Word of God should be explained by four methods, known by their initials as "PaRDeS," i.e. Peshat Remez Derash Sod. The *Peshat* is the simple explanation, i.e. it means what it says, in plain language. *Remez* ("hints") is the allusion and allegorical sense. *Derash* is the way the Midrash expounds the Bible (the homiletical way) and *Sod* (mystery) is the way the Kabbalah interprets the Bible.

Some of the exegetes used only one of these four ways, some used all the four ways in their exposition of the Bible.

As a whole their exposition tallies with that of the Christian exponents.

In modern times when Jews began to use the language of the land where they sojourned there were published translations into the vernacular, mostly in German and English.

CHAPTER XI

THE TALMUD AND THE MIDRASH[1]

After the great calamities which befell the Jewish people by
the destruction of Jerusalem, A.D. 70, Jewish learning found two
places of retreat. One was on the shores of the Euphrates in Babylon, the other in the little town of Jamnia, or Yavneh in Palestine.
This Jamnia school was in a subsequent period removed to Tiberias on the shores of the Sea of Galilee. About the year A.D. 230,
Rabbi Yehudah Hanasi compiled the *Mishna (Instruction);* a collection of Jewish laws and usages up to that time. This book
served later as basis for the Talmud. Just as the Mishna was supposed to be an explanation of the Mosaic Laws (the Bible) so
the Mishna itself had to be explained. The explanatory remarks
and opinions of the later Rabbis were compiled about a century
afterward by Rabbi Yehochanan who was then the Principal of
the Tiberias College. This new compilation was called *Gemara*
("Completion"). This Mishna and Gemara together was denomi-
nated *The Jerusalem Talmud.*

While this compilation of laws and their exposition was going on in downtrodden Judea, the more prosperous Jews of Meso-
potamia produced their own Gemara. This compilation which was
completed about A.D. 512 is called *Talmud Bavli* (Babylonian
Talmud). Although the Jerusalem Talmud was the simpler and
clearer, it did not appeal to the Jewish mind in diaspora as did the
more difficult and complex *Babel* Talmud. It is this Talmud that
became dominant in Jewish life and changed it radically.

This Babel Talmud is veritably a Babel (mixture) of laws and
customs, of facts and fiction, of science and superstitions. You may
start out with a simple discussion of a certain law and soon find
yourself in a fairy-land. It is hard to discern where reality ends
and imagination begins: where begins the *Halacha,* the study of the

[1] See chapter on "Literature."

law, and where ends the *Agada* (or Haggadah), the imaginative
or homiletic portion.

The language of the Talmud (mostly Aramaic), the style, the
method, the sequence of things, in short, everything seems tangled,
confused, chaotic, so that only years of instruction and practice
and a "Jewish head" may make one understand it. In the course
of time, the text of the Talmud became wedged in various commentaries, chiefly that of RASHI (short for *R*Abbi *SH*lomo *I*zchaki,
who was also the best known commentator on the Bible) printed
side by side with the text. These commentaries, glosses and anno-
tations help the student to unravel the obscure and entangled arguments of the Talmudical discussions.

Let us take, as example, the Sabbath. The Bible forbids all
work on that day. Now one may ask, what is "work"? Is sweep-
ing the floor, or cooking a meal, or washing the dishes, etc., called
"work," and thus should not be done on the Sabbath? If the
Rabbis had acted in the spirit of our Lord, who said that the Sabbath was for man and not man for the Sabbath, they might have
answered that question with a page or two. Instead, they wrote
a voluminous book called *Shabath,* wherein various kinds of human actions are discussed and disputed, before it is finally decided as to whether they are to be considered "work" or not. Thus
hundreds of laws concerning the Sabbath rest were evolved. A
great many of these laws involved the penalty of death if broken.
Now, in between the discussion of the various laws there are interspersed moral precepts, exegeses of certain verses in the Bible,
legends, some medicine, some astrology, ghost stories and many
other things which are entirely irrelevant. Some of the stories
may have some hidden secret truth, perhaps something which could
only be hinted but not plainly expressed. But all of them, even
the most absurd, have been considered by observant Jews as
sacred and infallible and obligatory.

During the Middle Ages, the Church held the Talmud responsible for Jewish stubbornness in refusing to accept the pre-
dominant religion. They accused the Talmud of depraving the
Jewish intellect and undermining their moral principles. Heavy
fines and imprisonment were imposed on those who kept the
Talmud in their house. Sometimes, these books were hunted out
and burned at the stake, in the hope that they would totally disappear and be no more a stumbling block to anyone. But the
cruelty and stupidity of the church-leaders had the reverse effect.

The more the Talmud was calumniated, the more the Jews loved it, preserved it and studied it, until it became the real "Torah" for the Jewish people. The *Bible*, by which name the Pentateuch is generally known, is considered, indeed, a most sacred book which ought to be recited periodically, but it is the *Talmud* which guides and directs Jewish life because only the Rabbis are authorized to interpret the Bible.

In their great zeal for the preservation of the Holy Book, in their care that no harm befall it, the Rabbis have built around their beloved books, hedges and fences, and locked it with several keys, so that the Bible — especially the Spirit of it — has become inaccessible. The Talmud is an impenetrable wall encircling and concealing the Bible. So the wall without has become sacred while the Holy Scriptures within have become obscure, forgotten, a "sealed book."

Jesus said: "Neither do men light a candle, and put it under a bushel, but on a candlestick," so that it gives light to all around it. The Rabbis did just the reverse: they put the light of the Word of God under a bushel, probably to keep it safe there, forgetting that the purpose of light is not to be kept safe, but to shine and keep the people safe and enlightened.

There are other books of ancient date which are considered as in line with the Talmud. Such is the *Midrash* ("exposition"). It is mostly *Haggadah*, homiletic interpretation of the Pentateuch. It also contains various stories, fables, allegories — sometimes to expound a passage in the Bible, sometimes just to inculcate some moral lesson. The various *Midrashim* form quite a large set of books in haggadic literature.

Then there are Apocryphal Appendices to the Talmud, such as: *Avoth d'Rabbi Nathan, Derech Eretz, Kalla* and others. Parables, stories, maxims, proverbs, folk-lore, fables, etc., find untrammelled expression in this vast collection, which has enjoyed great popularity among the Jews.

For the missionary to the Jews, it is interesting to know that the *Midrashim* reveal that various passages of the Old Testament which the New Testament applies to the Messiah were also applied to the Messiah by the Jews of old — for example, Isaiah 52:12-Isaiah 53, which later Jewish commentators applied to the Jewish people. The Midrash, like the New Testament, *referred it to the suffering Messiah*. According to the New Testament (Matthew 22:44 and in other parts of the New Testament) Psalm 110:1 is applied to the Messiah. Later modern rabbis made various efforts to suppress the old Jewish exegesis of passages which were favorable to the claims of Christianity but the Midrash on the Psalms interprets Psalm 18:36 thus: "Rabbi Judah in the name of Rabbi Chama says: that in the time to come, the Holy One — blessed be He! — will make King Messiah sit at His right hand, as it is said (Psalm 110:1), The Lord said unto my lord sit thou on my right hand, etc."

The Talmud being so voluminous, so difficult, it could not become the heritage of the mass of the Jewish people, especially not for the Jews who settled in European countries, and the Aramaic language, in which most of the Talmud was written, became foreign and difficult to study. Thus there arose the new danger that the laws and usages of the Talmud would be forgotten. To meet this exigency, new compilations of the laws came into being. These ·compilations were written in plain Hebrew, systematically arranged, leaving out all the legends, etc., of the Talmud, so that all Jews could more easily read them.

On these compilations read chapter on Literature, Section: *"Codification."*

CHAPTER XII

THE KABBALAH

This mystic philosophy, an offshoot of Judaism, has had an immense influence upon the Jewish people for hundreds of years. It took a firm hold of the people in connection with the Messianic movement[1] and it spread widely with the rise of Chassidism in the eighteenth century.

Today there is little interest left among Jews in the Kabbalah. Yet, because of the indelible imprint it left on Judaism, and because much of its mysticism may be likened to Christian mysticism, it is but fitting to devote to it, at least, a short chapter here.[2]

The word Kabbalah is derived from the Hebrew root Kabbel, which signifies "to receive." It has been used in a large sense, as comprehending all the explications, maxims and rituals which the Jews have *received* from their fathers. But it is more often employed to designate a particular species of theology and philosophy. It is especially that mystical exposition of the Bible and metaphysical speculations concerning God and other beings (angels, etc.) which are found in many Jewish authors, and which are said to have been handed down by secret tradition from the earliest ages. It has been pretended by its adherents that Moses received it on Mount Sinai, but for various reasons he revealed it to a select few only. Many of the Kabbalistic books were attributed to ancient venerable authorship; for example, there is the book "Raziel" (a name of an angel — meaning "Mystery of God"). This was supposed to be a gift which Adam, the first man, received from the angel by that name. Another book was attributed to the Patriarch Abraham.

The most celebrated of these books are *Sepher Yetsirah* (Book of Creation), and the *Zohar* (Splendor). The Book of Creation

---

[1] The Kabbalah had a profound influence on the pseudo-Messianic movement of Shabathai Zvi.

[2] See also chapter on "Literature: Kabbalistic Books."

was supposed to have been written by Abraham. Some attributed its authorship to Rabbi Akivah, while the author of the Zohar was said to be Rabbi Shimeon Bar Yochai, a disciple of R. Akivah. These two rabbis, who lived at the time of the Bar Kochvah uprising in the second century A.D., have been considered as great saints and highly venerated.[3]

Literary critics ascribe the appearance of the "Book of Creation" (by an unknown author) to between the seventh and ninth centuries, while the Zohar (the Kabbalistic interpretation of the Pentateuch) was probably written by Moshe de Leon about 1290 A.D. The rise of the Kabbalah took place at the time of the Maimonidean (Rambam) Philosophical controversy in Judaism, and was caused thereby.

The Zohar has exercised a profound influence on late Judaism. The mystics devoted much of their time to the study of this book. Others, for example the Yemenite Jews, have been "reading" it, just as some Jews were reading or "saying" Thillim. One may find in this book, and Kabbalah as a whole, much of Christian dogma, such as the Trinity, the fall of angels, original sin, eternal punishment of the wicked, and even of the incarnation and deity of the Messiah.

According to Kabbalah the goal of religion and of union with the Creator can be attained not by obeying the Law nor by philosophical speculation but only through the contemplation of the mystic tradition which goes back to the origins of mankind. It taught that the Infinite One (En-sof) did not create the world directly but that an emanation from Him created the world. From this first emanation there came others — altogether ten in number, or in the language of the Kabbalah, ten "Sephiroth." By these emanations God clothes Himself in a body and makes Himself visible. By them He communicates with His creatures, and by them He directs the universe.

These ten "Sephiroth," which have finite and infinite attributes, serve also as intermediaries between Creator and created. God revealed Himself to Israel selecting it as His people to preserve the world. The laws and ceremonies of Judaism have a profound mystical significance. The earthly Temple at Jerusalem had its counterpart in the heavenly Temple. When it was destroyed

[3] Thousands of Jews annually visit their graves in Palestine to pray for their intercession before the Throne of Mercy.

prayer took its place. Thus prayer is essential to the existence of the world.

The Kabbalah has much to say about the soul and its transmigration but we do not think it worthwhile to enlarge upon it here.

Kabbalah influenced many Christian theologians who sought and found confirmation of Christian dogmas and doctrines in the teachings of Kabbalah, such as the Trinity, the Incarnation of God in Jesus, the fall of the angels, original sin, eternal punishment. (Pope Sixtus, 1471-84, favored the production of Latin translations of various Kabbalah books, to be used in defending the Catholic faith.)

Some mystics used, or rather abused, the Kabbalah for "practical" purposes, by applying certain formulae, composed of names of God and angels and the like (meaningless hocus-pocus) in amulets and charms against evil spirits, to avert illness, or to heal it, as a whole to help the bearer of such a Kabbalah talisman or charm to achieve his desires.

Many of the "wonder-rabbis" of the Chassidim were famed for their miracles which were supposedly also performed by such charms. This may have given impetus to the spread of Chassidism, and this also may have been the main cause of its decline and fall.

CHAPTER XIII

THE MESSIAH

In our introduction we spoke of the difficulties the missionary encounters when preaching the Gospel to Jews. But there are also many advantages in Jewish evangelization, because of the basic principles common to both Christian and Jew, such as the common conception of God, the common belief in the Bible and the Messiah.

These three beliefs are unknown to the heathen in foreign mission work, while with the Jews, these beliefs are the essence not only of their faith but also of their very existence as Jews.

Next to God nothing occupies the Jewish religious mind as does the Messiah. The various daily prayers, at the synagogue and at home, revolve around this axis — the Messiah.

It is the old, old story, and they believe it. They believe that God had chosen Israel to be a holy people, a "kingdom of priests" — to be a blessing to all the peoples of the earth. He was very strict in the training of them toward the fulfilling of that divine mission. Whenever they disobeyed Him, He chastised them severely by raising enemies ("whips of His wrath") against them. Then when they repented and pleaded for His forgiveness He raised unto them "redeemers" (Judges and Kings) who helped them against their enemies. Whether they implicitly believe it, or only have a beclouded idea of it, it is in every Jew's conscience. It lies deep in his heart.

He, more than anyone else, sees that all through the Bible God never wanted to destroy them entirely as He destroyed other sinful rebellious people; He did not want to defeat His own purpose in His plan of salvation. So He always restored them to their senses, to their home, to their well-being. To make them conscious of their guilt and need of atonement He instituted the sacrifices. Thus God made it clear to them: "You, as individuals, and you as a nation, deserve to be punished by death, but I will overlook your

116

sins if you 'cover them' by the blood of an animal substitute." If he is learned in Jewish lore he also knows that several years (70) after the destruction of the First Temple God caused a Gentile King, Cyrus of Persia, to be a redeemer, a "messiah" to let the Jews return to their "Promised Land" and there serve God as ordained by Moses and the prophets, i.e. in the preparation toward the final goal of being a blessing to the world.

This preparatory schooling under the guidance of Ezra and Nehemiah and other enlightened and earnest teachers wrought wonderful changes in the hearts and minds of the Jewish people. Idolatry disappeared entirely. There was a genuine faith and love of God, a passion for justice, etc. But what he is not (usually) aware of is that the Rabbis in their mistaken zeal, zeal without knowledge, in course of time came to worship the letter that killeth and forsook the spirit that reviveth. It seems that when Satan could no longer beguile the chosen people with the worship of foreign gods, he tried, successfully, to confuse and falsify the worship of the true God. The greatest, the most fatal of these falsifications and adulterations was the conception of the *Messiah*. For some reason, mainly ignorance, fear or egotism, the leaders of the people, during the latter part of the Second Temple, found it expedient to blur the picture of the promised Redeemer. They should have known, and undoubtedly many did know, that the only purpose for electing their people, the only aim of the Covenants, beginning with Abraham, was to make them into a holy people of priests to teach the world the truth of God and that the culmination of the covenants was to be the coming of the Saviour of the world.

Abraham was shown, at the "offering" of Isaac, the Lamb for the greatest of all sacrifices (see Genesis 22:8, etc.). *Moses and the prophets foretold His coming.* Jeremiah announced the coming of the *New Covenant* in unequivocal language. Daniel predicted the exact date of His coming. Many of the Rabbis knew, and said, that all the prophets prophesied only to the time of the Messiah. They, the Rabbis, even deduced from the Bible that the Old Testament laws including the observance of the festivals were to be abrogated by the coming of the Messiah.

And yet when He came, they received Him not. They rejected Him. They had been teaching the people that the Messiah would come only to free them from the foreign yoke. They withheld from them the vision which the prophets saw, of a Messiah who would be Redeemer of all mankind. Thus when Jesus came, the

Rabbis pictured Him as an apostate to Judaism, a rebel against the invincible Roman power and therefore most dangerous. Thus He was delivered to the "powers that be," and executed as a dangerous criminal. This the average Jew does not exactly know.

Divine retribution was not slow in coming. The Jewish people, who rejected Him who wanted to make them *free*, were driven into exile, their capital city destroyed, and the Temple, the altar, the priesthood, and with them the sacrificial rites to "cover up sin," came to an end.

Had this calamity happened to any other nation, the nation itself would have come to an end. Not so with Israel. God is not through with the nation yet. He destined them to be an everlasting nation. They have yet to serve Him, to fulfill His mission. But while not utterly destroyed, they have nevertheless experienced by His chastening, one catastrophe after another. As Moses foretold: the horrors of the day would make them pray for the night, and the terrors of the night make them wish for the day to come. Of this the Jews are well aware although the picture is not yet clear. It is partial blindness that obscures the real picture.

No wonder that most of their solemn and fervent prayers are for the coming of the Messiah, not only to redeem them from their bondage and the misery that is involved in it but, more so, because the Messiah would restore the sacrifices and so "cover up sin." The observant Jew, throughout exile, has firmly believed that only the priestly sacrifices are valid to atone for sin, and all they could do, in prayer, repentance, charity and studying the Torah, was obviously only a temporary substitute.

This consciousness of guilt and need for a means of atonement is expressed in nearly all the prayers during week-days and especially so on the Sabbath and Feast Days.

At the beginning of the daily morning prayers God is invoked to remember His oath to Abraham who was ready to sacrifice his beloved son. Afterward the chapter ordering the daily sacrifices is read (Numbers 28:1-8). Then there is to be recited a certain chapter of the Talmud (Mishnah, Treatise Zevachim, chapter 5) which deals with the locations of the various sacrifices, the use of their blood, etc. After reading several passages of the Bible, mostly Psalms, there follows the most solemn part of the three daily services — the so-called "Eighteen" (eighteen benedictions) which is recited standing and silently. Before rising up the worshiper pleads: "O Rock of Israel, arise to the help of Israel, and deliver according to thy promise, Judah and Israel. Our Redeemer the Lord of Hosts is His name, the Holy One of Israel. Blessed art thou, O Lord, who has redeemed Israel." The greater part of the "Eighteen" is supplication for the national redemption and welfare of Israel. Thus for example: "Look upon our affliction and plead our cause, and redeem us speedily for thy name's sake; for thou art a mighty Redeemer. Blessed art thou, O Lord, the Redeemer of Israel."

"Sound the great horn for our freedom; lift up the ensign to gather our exiles, and gather us from the four corners of the earth. Blessed art thou, O Lord, who gatherest the banished ones of the people Israel."

"And to Jerusalem, thy city, return in mercy, and dwell therein, as thou hast spoken; rebuild it soon in our days as an everlasting building, and speedily set up therein the throne of David. Blessed art thou, O Lord, the rebuilder of Jerusalem."

"The offspring of David thy servant speedily cause to flourish and let his horn be exalted by thy salvation, because we wait for thy salvation all the day. . . ."

"And let our eyes behold thy return to Zion in mercy. Blessed art thou, O Lord, who restoreth thy divine presence[1] unto Zion."

After the "Eighteen" there comes the prayer that God may speedily rebuild the temple where they might serve Him with the offerings that would please Him as in ancient years.

On New-Moons and feast days there is an additional prayer that God may remember the Messiah son of David.

There is a shortened form of the "Eighteen" for those who on account of illness or some weighty reason cannot recite the full form. This shortened form really shows us what is the quintessence of the Jewish prayer.

I quote it here in full:

"Give us understanding, O Lord our God, to know thy ways; circumcise our hearts to fear thee, and forgive us so that we may be redeemed. Keep us far from sorrow; and satiate us on the pastures of thy land, and gather our scattered ones from the four corners of the earth. Let the righteous rejoice in the rebuilding of thy city, and in the establishment of thy temple, and in the flourishing of the horn of David thy servant, and in the light of the son of Jesse, Thine *Anointed* (Messiah). Even before we call, do thou answer. Blessed art thou who hearkenest unto prayer."

[1] In Hebrew: Thy "Shekinah."

Toward the end of the morning prayer there are these lines:
"And a Redeemer shall come to Zion and to them that turn from transgression in Jacob, saith the Lord: And as for me, this is my covenant with them, saith the Lord: my Spirit that is upon thee, and my words which I have put in thy mouth, shall not depart out of thy mouth, nor out of the mouth of thy seed, nor out of the mouth of thy seed's seed, saith the Lord, from now and forever" (taken from Isaiah 59:20, 21).

On holy days (Sabbath, New Moon, etc.), on the days when during the existence of the Temple additional sacrifices were offered, extra prayers are now recited, confessing that on account of *"our" sins* "we" have been exiled and thus not being able to bring the prescribed sacrifices, therefore "we" implore God not for our sake (for we are not worthy) but for your name's sake, and for the sake of the covenant with the forefathers — to bring us back to our land and there we will again offer the prescribed sacrifices.

This yearning for redemption, for forgiveness of sin, is felt and uttered not only in the liturgy of the daily services but on various other occasions. Thus, the lengthy prayer ("grace") which is recited after meals is saturated with that longing. From among many such passages let us quote this:

"May the All-merciful make us worthy of the days of the Messiah, and of the life of the world to come. Great salvation giveth He to His king, and showeth lovingkindness to His Messiah, to David and to his seed forevermore. . . ."

And not only in prayer, which is performed several times every day, but also, in common parlance, is this longing for the Redeemer, the Mashiah, given expression.

In short, the belief, the yearning, and expectancy in the speedy coming of the Messiah, has exerted the greatest influence upon the life and customs of the Jewish people. Throughout the centuries of misery, humiliation and persecution in exile, the "coming of Messiah" has been the greatest consolation and most treasured hope.

No article of faith is recited with so much fervor and devotion as this: "I believe with perfect faith in the coming of the Messiah, and though he tarry, I will wait daily for his coming."

What is the Jewish conception of the person of the Messiah? Well, there is no consistent or uniform picture of the Messiah. The Jewish sages differed widely in their portrayal of the Redeemer, depending on the times and places, and the material and cultural position of their people. There is thus much confusion about the Messiah. Some thought of Him as a divine all-powerful person who would perform great miracles and introduce great changes in nature. Others thought and taught that He would be human although endowed with extraordinary powers and qualities. Maimonides (RAMBAM), who formulated the "articles of faith," teaches that "There is no difference between this world and the days of the Messiah except subjection of Kingdoms."

We have already seen, in the chapter on religion, that Maimonides often contradicted himself. He was a rationalist and did not believe that anything is supernatural or is not in accordance with previous human experience. On the other hand he was a faithful follower of the rabbis and he enjoined the people to observe all their laws and teachings with all the irrationalism and the absurdities it involved.

If the Jew is to believe Maimonides the rationalist, that the Messiah is just as human as human can be, how is he to believe Maimonides the rabbinic dogmatist, that he is to expect daily the Messiah's coming? How can He come today or tomorrow? Does He not have first to be born and grow up in a natural way?

Or was He born already? When? Where? Where is He now, He who may at any moment arrive (according to that same Maimonides)?

Well, the Jewish people are quite confused in their belief in the Messiah, as in many other beliefs, because the rabbis have confused them, for various reasons. Generally the Jews who were born and reared into ages-old tradition firmly believed in the Messiah as superhuman, as divine. We have seen that in the daily prayers the Redeemer is sometimes referred to as God, sometimes as "Son of David" sent by God. No doubt the Jewish people throughout the ages have harbored the thought, the vision, though not a clear one, of the Messiah being God incarnate.

The "Targums," the translations and interpretations of the Bible, that have been used in the synagogues since ancient times (see "Targum") have the same conception of the Messiah as is to be found in the New Testament. Those passages in the Old Testament which in the New Testament are applied to the Messiah are also interpreted so in the Targums.

The fact that the Targums have been held sacred and printed side by side with the Hebrew text, and read every Sabbath, according to old usage, clearly proves that the Messiah was held by the ancient rabbis, and the people in general, as being divine in human form.

In the "Benediction of the Moon" (recited monthly) the worshiper shouts: "David King of Israel lives and exists" and the prayer is finished with the verse, "And they shall seek Jehovah their God and David their king, Amen" (Hosea 3:5).

Young people in Israel have a popular dance which is accompanied by singing continuously, "David king of Israel lives and exists." This is sung in a rapturous manner quite often on various occasions. Does it not show that the belief in the supernatural Messiah is still deeply ingrained in the Jewish heart?

Moreover, ever since the restoration of the State of Israel, the Jewish people still wait for the Messiah. They still pray the same old prayers for God's return to Zion. Nothing in Jewish liturgy referring to redemption physical and spiritual, has been changed, although many Jewish leaders demanded changes. The people still wait for the miraculous, for the divine Messiah.

What have the people been expecting throughout the exile? The answers are various. The prayers during the weekdays, and more so on holydays, expressed the main yearning for the return to Zion in order to be able to serve God, as ordained in the Old Testament by bloody sacrifices, which may be done only at the Holy Temple in Jerusalem. The coming of the Messiah was also to inaugurate the Kingdom of Heaven, sometimes called "Kingdom of Shaddai," with Zion as its center.

His coming is also associated with "resurrection of the dead" and the "Day of Judgment." All these events are often included in the name "Olam Habba," the world to come.

While some of the Rabbis portrayed this "Coming World" as pure spiritual bliss, others pictured it as a paradise, where and when men, mainly Jews, will live pleasantly and where they might obtain all the innocent, harmless pleasures of life without the need of any exertion to obtain them. Delicious food, as well as beautiful clothes, will be produced by the earth ready to be used, according to Talmud: Sabbath 30b and Ketuboth 111b. There will be banquets where the righteous one will partake of the meat of the mythical wild ox, and the fish Leviathan, and imbibe the wine which is preserved for them since the six days of creation.

These beliefs and hopes of Olam Habba (Eschatology) are closely knit also with the immortality of the soul which after leaving the body is purified in purgatory (in Gehenna) and then ascends into Paradise ("Gan Eden") where it lives in bliss till the coming of Messiah and the resurrection.

Now, as mentioned previously, these ideas are quite confused, but they all revolve around the Messiah who *lives* and waits for the opportune time for His appearance.

Where is He? Some Rabbis said that He is now in "Gan Eden" (Paradise). Some said that He is living disguised in Rome. Some said that He is the "Shechinah" which is in exile, wherever the Jewish people sojourn.

Explaining the beginning of verse 3, chapter 30 of Deuteronomy, which may be translated: "And He will return with thy returning . . . ," the Talmud Meggilah 29a says that this teaches that the Holy One is in exile together with His people and together with them, He, too, will return. In other words, when He redeems His people, He Himself will be redeemed with them. When is the Messiah to come? There is no uniform answer to this question. To sum up the various opinions of the Rabbis it may be said that there has been a specified time for His coming but this set time might be hastened or postponed in accordance with the worthiness of the people.

Many Rabbis tried to figure out the appointed time of His coming, but as ever, were disappointing. It often even led to disaster. Often usurpers, scoundrels, or half-witted men assumed the role of the Messiah and thus misled the people into great calamities. Jewish history has many tragic accounts of such false Messiahs.

Christians witnessing to Jews, and the Jewish people have thus a subject in common and to both it is of the most vital interest. (See chapter, "How to Identify the Messiah.")

CHAPTER XIV

CHANGING ATTITUDE OF THE JEWS TOWARD JESUS

Jesus came to His own, but His own received Him not.

We know that the masses of the people followed Him faithfully, lovingly, reverently, but when the crisis, the climax came, when He was to taste the bitter cup, He was alone; even His most faithful disciple, Peter, denied Him for a while. For a moment it seemed that even the Father forsook Him. Incited by the leaders, whose leadership was obviously jeopardized by Jesus, some people who yesterday shouted "Hosannah," now shouted, "Crucify Him"!

After the Resurrection, thousands came back to Him, *then hundreds of thousands,* both in Judea and in Diaspora. But the Jewish people as a whole, "received Him not." Not even when their Temple and the Holy City were destroyed and the majority of the people were either destroyed or dispersed — all as Jesus foretold; not even then did the blind leaders relinquish their grip on the people, keeping them away from their Saviour. In order to justify their crime against Jesus, they concocted various tales to portray Jesus as an impostor, a blasphemer, a traitor, a sorcerer, who fully deserved the death to which the "saintly" Rabbis condemned Him. These tales, though so self-contradictory, so farfetched in imagination and so perverted and distorted, were propagated and handed down from generation to generation both orally and in script, and sad as it is strange, the people implicitly believed these wild yarns. The shrewd leaders knew how to keep away anything that might contradict their story. The New Testament or any authentic account of the life of Jesus was nowhere within reach.

Excommunication was the fate of anyone guilty of reading any Christian book, let alone one who dared believe or speak favorably of Christ. Worst of all, the life and acts of the so-called "Christian people" could only serve the Rabbis as an example of how bad Christianity was. The Roman (Catholic) Church in the

Middle Ages surely could not serve as a good example of what Christianity is meant to be.

However, the impact of the Christian Reformation upon Europe had its effect also on the Jewish people. Protestantism became interested in the Scriptures — both the Old Testament and the New Testament — and consequently the Jewish people appeared to Christians in a new light. They began to realize that both the Old and the New Covenants were made primarily with the Jewish people and were to be everlasting covenants.

People began to see the Jews, not as a God-forsaken, accursed rabble, but as those who were the chosen people, and thus were worth saving, and worthy of Christian love. The Jews, many of them, could not help but reciprocate. They began to see that the Roman Church, with its Inquisition and persecution of Jews, was not synonymous with Christianity. Some even dared to read the New Testament which, after the Reformation, could more easily be obtained. And, of course, anyone who read the New Testament, or even part of it, could no longer believe the incongruous, incoherent and scurrilous tales about Jesus. Then, with the bursting of that bubble, the outlines of the true Jesus began to be recognized by the Jewish mind. But, alas! the risk was still too great to utter what one thought of Jesus, if it was not in strict accordance with the utterance of the ancient rabbis.

Now and then, however, there were courageous men who dared utter some praise of Jesus, and of course they suffered the consequences. Such men were, to cite but a few outstanding instances:

Baruch Spinoza, considered as the greatest Jewish philosopher and, by many, as one of the greatest philosophers mankind has ever produced. He lived in Protestant Holland, 1632-1677. He was excommunicated by the rabbis of his hometown, Amsterdam. Recently many people in Israel have voiced their conviction that the rabbis ought now to remove that excommunication. The Israeli Prime Minister, Ben Gurion, is a great and outspoken admirer of Spinoza. In his "Tractatus Theologica-Politicus," Spinoza writes:

"Christ was not so much a prophet as the mouthpiece of God, Christ was sent to teach not only Jews, but the whole human race; and therefore it was not enough that his mind should be accommodated to the opinions of the Jews alone, but also to the opinion and fundamental teaching common to the whole human race; in other words, to ideas universal and truth."

Heinrich Graetz, the greatest of Jewish historians (lived in Germany, 1817-1891), writes:

"High-minded earnestness and spotless moral purity were his undeniable attributes . . . the gentle disposition and humility of Jesus reminds one of Hillel, whom he seems to have taken as his particular model, and whose golden rule, 'What you wish not to be done to yourself do not unto others,' he adopted as the starting point of his moral code. Like Hillel, Jesus looked on the promotion of peace and forgiveness of injuries as the highest forms of virtue. His whole being was permeated by that deeper religion which contributed to the mildness of his face. He has made humanity honour; he has carried the highest wisdom to the homes of the lowly and the ignorant of the world. He has carried it beyond all barriers of schools and temples, and for this, only, he had to die a death of shame. The redeemer of the poor, the teacher of the ignorant, the friend of all that faint with toil and are oppressed with cares must die on the cross. Over the supreme tragedy let the angel of sorrow spread his wings. Veil thy face, sun! Be darkened, sky! Let the earth tremble and men mourn in tears! The most angelic of men, the most loving of teachers, the meek and humble prophet is to die by the death of the cross" (*History of the Jews,* Vol, II ,p. 149).

Dr. J. M. Jost, 1793-1860, another great Jewish historian, writes:

"Spotless walk, unselfish love for mankind. Thousands of Jews adored Jesus, their teacher and friend" (*The History of Judaism and Their Sects,* Vol. I, Chapter 12).

Benjamin Disraeli, the Earl of Beaconfield (1804-1881), novelist and statesman (British Prime Minister), writes:

"The pupil of Moses may ask himself whether all the princes of the House of David have done so much for the Jews as that Prince who was crucified. . . . Had it not been for him, the Jews would have been comparatively unknown or known only as a high Oriental Caste which had lost its country. Has not he made their history the most famous history in the world?

"The wildest dreams of their rabbis have been far exceeded. Has not Jesus conquered Europe and changed its name to Christendom? All countries that refuse the cross will, and the time will come when the countless myriads in America and Australia will find music in the songs of Zion, and solace in the parables of Galilee."

Theodore Reinach (1860-1928), of France, another great Jewish historian and archeologist of renown, writes:

"Although we know very little with certainty concerning the

life and teachings of Christ, we know enough of him to believe that, in morals as well as in theology, he was the heir and continuator of the old prophets of Israel. There is no necessary gap between Isaiah and Jesus, but it is the misfortune of both Judaism and Christianity that a gap has been affected by the infiltration of of heathen ideas in the one, and the stubborn 'only too explainable' reluctance of the other to admit among its prophets one of its greatest sons. I consider it the duty of both enlightened Christians and Jews to endeavor to bridge over this gap."

Max Nordau (1849-1823), author of international fame, Zionist leader and colleague of Dr. Herzl, writes:

"Jesus is the soul of our soul as he is the flesh of our flesh. Who then could think of excluding him from the people of Israel? St. Peter will remain the only Jew who said of the Son of David: 'I know not the man.' If the Jews up to the present have not rendered homage to the sublime beauty of the figure of Jesus, it is because their tormentors have always persecuted, tortured, and assassinated them in his name."

Albert Einstein, the world-famous scientist, expressed his opinion about Jesus in an interview recorded in *The Saturday Evening Post,* as follows:

"To what extent are you influenced by Christianity?"

"As a child," Einstein said, "I received instructions both in the Bible and in the Talmud. I am a Jew, but am enthralled by the luminous figure of the Nazarene."

"Have you read Emil Ludwig's book on Jesus?"

"Emil Ludwig's Jesus is shallow," Einstein replied. "Jesus is too colossal for the pen of phrase-mongers, however artful. No man can dispose of Christianity with a *bon mot.*"

"You accept the historical existence of Jesus?"

"Unquestionably. No man can read the Gospels without feeling the actual presence of Jesus. His personality pulsates in every word. No myth is filled with such life. How different, for instance, is the impression which we receive from an account of the legendary heroes of antiquity like Theseus! Theseus and other heroes of his type lack the authentic vitality of Jesus."

"Ludwig Lewisohn, in one of his recent books, claims that many of the sayings of Jesus paraphrase the sayings of other prophets," Viereck interposed.

"No man," Einstein replied, "can deny the fact that Jesus existed, nor that his sayings are beautiful. Even if some of them have been said before, no one expressed them so divinely as he."

Israel Zangwill, considered as the greatest novelist in English Jewish literature, says: "We shall never get the future straight until we disentangle the past. To disentangle the past means to re-examine the trial of Jesus — myths woven purposely by our leaders around the greatest and most noble personality in history, only that we may not see and recognize the real Jesus. To us, my brethren, in this our day, is given the privilege to reclaim the Christ we have lost for so many centuries. Has not the crucified Christ more than fulfilled the highest and noblest of our greatest prophets? Is not He the Incarnation of the essence of what the Law, the Psalms and the Prophets taught?"

Dr. Claude Montefiore, recognized spokesman of English Liberals, President of the Jewish Religious Union, speaking of Jesus, said:

"The most important Jew that has ever lived, to whom the sinner and the outcast, age after age, have owed a great debt of gratitude" (*Jewish Chronicle,* July 14, 1809).

"I cannot conceive that a time will come when the figure of Jesus will no longer be a star of the first magnitude in the spiritual heavens, when he will no longer be regarded as one of the greatest religious heroes and teachers the world has seen. I cannot conceive that a time will come when 'the Bible' in the eyes of Europe will no longer be composed of the Old Testament and the New, or when the Gospels will be less prized than the Pentateuch, or the Books of the Chronicles preferred to the Epistles of Paul. The religion of the future will be, as I believe, a developed and purified Judaism, but from that developed and purified Judaism the records will tell, however imperfectly, of perhaps its greatest teacher. Certainly its most potent and influential teacher will not be excluded."

The following most remarkable tribute to Christ appeared in a conservative Jewish periodical:

"I have often thought that Christians miss much of the glory and the grandeur and the beauty of the life of the founder of their faith, his wonderful power of imagery, his remarkable homiletic gifts, the magnificent doctrine he taught and the splendid life he lived by way of example to his followers . . . rebelled and revolted against the infamous ecclesiastical system that prevailed in the days of Jesus as well as against the political conditions which he denounced. There must, too, have been in his character, in his life, much more than in his death something infinitely glorious for him to have become, largely among Jews be it remembered, the object of such adoration as was paid him years and years after his death" (from *Jewish Chronicle*, June 5, 1931).

Dr. Felix Adler, founder of Ethical Culture Societies, speaking in New York before a large Jewish audience, had this to say:

"It has been said that if Christ came to New York or Chicago, they would stone him in the very churches. It is not so! If Christ came to New York or Chicago the publicans and sinners would sit at his feet! For they would know that he cared for them better than they in their darkness knew how to care for themselves, and would love him as they loved him in the days of yore."

He goes on to point out that the resurrection of Jesus must have some historical foundation to have survived the centuries.

"It is sometimes insinuated that the entire Christian religion depends on the accounts contained in the New Testament, purporting that Jesus actually rose on the third day and was seen by his followers; and that if these reports are found to be contradictory, unsupported by sufficient evidence, and in themselves incredible, then the bottom falls out of the belief in immortality, as represented by Christianity."

He continued:

"But similar reports have arisen in the world time and again; apparitions of the dead have been seen and have been taken for real; and yet such stories, after being current for a time, invariably have passed into oblivion. Why did this particular story persist, despite the paucity and the insufficiency of the evidence? Why did it get itself believed and take root?"

These glowing words coming from a man of international reputation shocked some of his rationalistic admirers, who charged him with having surrendered to the orthodox Christian position.

Here is the opinion of one of the outstanding rabbis of France, *Rabbi Emmanuel Weill:*

"Let us then as Jews be thankful there was a Jesus and a Paul. I do not know the secret of God, but I believe that Jesus and Christianity were providential means, useful to the Deity in guiding all men gradually and by an effort, keeping pace with the mental state of the majority of men, from paganism up to the pure and true idea of the divinity."

And here one of Italy, *Prof. David Castelli:*

"Jesus, in a certain sense, fulfilled in his person the prophecies of the Old Testament: they reached in him a height beyond which it is impossible to go. He was the great teacher of mankind, spreading among all nations the principle of love and humanity which, until then, had remained confined within the limits of Judaism."

American rabbis, living in a free Christian civilization, could also freely express what they thought of Jesus, and they often did. Thus a rabbi in St. Louis opened the service by reading the Sermon on the Mount and then preached a sermon giving the following six reasons why Jews should acknowledge Jesus:

1. "Because he lived as a Jew, mingled with Jews, and observed their festivals."
2. "He died as a Jewish patriot, for principle and convictions."
3. "His religion was the religion of the Synagogue. He taught the Fatherhood of God and the Brotherhood of man."
4. "Jesus was a Jew in his criticism of the Jews of his day."
5. "Jesus was a Jew in that he influenced the Jewish race by his personality. In other words, because Jesus was a kinsman of the Jews, they became of world importance."
6. "Jesus was a Jew in his influence on the history of humanity."

Rabbi Stephen S. Wise, of New York, a great Zionist leader, one of the most prominent leaders of American Jewry, was often attacked (by certain speakers and writers) on account of his favorable expressions about Jesus. In a sermon at the civic Lenten Service held under the auspices of the Petterson Council of Churches, he is quoted as saying:

"There is less difference than most people think in the creeds of Christians and Jews. We differ only in the way in which we place Christ. He is a wonderful Jew. He is my teacher as well as yours. It would be well for everyone, Jew and Gentile alike, to follow the teachings of Jesus Christ."

In an article that appeared in *The Outlook,* June 7, 1913, Rabbi Wise says: "It is no mean joy and ignoble pride in us of the House of Israel to recognize, to honor and to cherish among our brothers — Jesus the Jew."

Rabbi Krauskopf, of Philadelphia:

"I will yield to none in recognizing the civilizing influence of the Man of Nazareth. I am ready to bestow upon him as high a tribute as anyone has yet bestowed" (from *A Rabbi's Impressions*).

Dr. Gerson B. Levi, of Chicago, in a sermon published in the *Chicago Tribune:*

"A protest of Orthodox Jews criticizing me for my position has led me to make this public statement. For some time I have been teaching in my classes at the Temple, the New Testament with special reference to the life of Jesus in the Gospels and the

Acts of the Apostles, giving the history of the founding of the Christian Church. This is a Christian civilization and the majority of the people of America are of the Christian faith. Therefore, I feel it the duty of everyone who would understand our present civilization to study the foundations upon which it rests."

Rabbi H. G. Enelow, D.D., of Temple of Emmanuel, New York City:

"Among the great and the good that the human race has produced, none has ever approached Jesus in universality of appeal and sway. He has become the most fascinating figure in history. In him is combined what is best and most mysterious and most enchanting in Israel — the eternal people whose child he was. The Jew cannot help glorying in what he has meant to the world, nor can he help hoping that Jesus may yet serve as a bond of union between Jew and Christian."

Rabbi Enelow asks and answers the question: "What does the modern Jew think of Jesus? A Prophet? Yes, crowning a great tradition, and who can compute all that Jesus has meant to humanity? The love he has inspired, the solace he has given, the good he has engendered, the hope and joy he has kindled — all that is unequaled in human history." He also speaks of Jesus as the most "fascinating and most influential and most beneficent religious teacher."

Dr. E. N. Cailisch, Richmond, Va., giving reasons why Jesus was excluded from Judaism, expressed regret because of the estrangement that has existed between Jesus and his people:

"This is a moderate and restrained expression of conditions, and to those who regret that this estrangement has existed between Jesus and his people, and who hold that there is much in his life and teachings which can be of value to the Jew, the 'hope must remain that somehow, and at some not too distant time, Jesus will be reclaimed by Judaism, and will assume the place which should be his in the minds and hearts of his fellow Jews.'"

"With this thought I am in hearty accord. An ancient rabbi once said: 'From all of my teachers I have learned,' and in our ritual we voice the prayer: 'O Lord, open our eyes that we may see and welcome all truth, whether shining from the annals of ancient revelations or reaching us through the seers of our own time.' In this spirit I agree with the writer that the time has come when the Jew of today shall seek to know if there is not something in the life and doctrine of Jesus of Nazareth that will help him to make his own life nobler and truer, whether or not there may be room for Jesus in modern Judaism even as he had place in the ancient synagogue."

Isidore Singer, Ph.D., Managing Editor of the Jewish Encyclopedia, expresses his views in the following words:

"I regard Jesus of Nazareth as a Jew of Jews, one whom all Jewish people are learning to love. His teachings have been an immense service to the world in bringing Israel's God to the knowledge of hundreds of millions of mankind."

The great change in Jewish thought concerning Jesus of Nazareth, I cannot better illustrate than by this fact: When I was a boy, had my father, who was a very pious man, heard the name of Jesus uttered from the pulpit of the synagogue, he and every other man in the congregation would have left the building and the rabbi would have been dismissed at once.

Now it is not strange in many synagogues to hear sermons preached eulogistic of this Jesus, and no one thinks of protesting; in fact, we are all glad to claim Jesus as one of our people.

I also wish to call attention to that masterly, monumental book written in Hebrew, *Jesus of Nazareth*, by Joseph Klausner, one of the greatest Hebrew scholars and professors in the Hebrew University of Palestine. This was the first life of Christ published in the Hebrew language, and, according to all critics, Jewish and Christian, it is a scholarly work of the first magnitude. It has done more to bring Israel nearer to Jesus than all the Medieval churches and to a great extent many of the Protestant churches even of today. Though it caused a great furor, the author was neither excommunicated nor stoned to death as might have been his lot in former days. For the first time in 1900 years, a rabbinical Jew discussed the life of Jesus. "He pitilessly destroyed the idea that Jesus was a myth. He tells his readers they are wrong in taking a negative or indifferent attitude to Jesus, for his character and his indisputable idealism deserve a positive valuation." He declares all the hostile passages about Christ in the Talmud possess no historical value; that likewise the book, *Toldoth Yeshu*, is unhistorical and blasphemous.

I quote from the last chapter of this book which has so greatly stirred the Jewish and Christian world: "But Jesus is for the Jewish nation a great Jewish teacher of morality and an artist in parable. In his ethical code, there is a sublimity, distinctiveness, and originality in form unparalleled in any other Hebrew ethical code; neither is there any parallel to the remarkable art of his parables. The shrewdness and sharpness of his proverbs and his forceful epigrams serve, in an exceptional degree, to make the ethical code be stripped of its wrappings of miracles and mysticism; the book of the ethics of Jesus will be one of the choicest treasures in the literature of Israel for all time."

I have quoted but a few rabbis and scholars of prominence, and these are of the past generation. Liberal rabbis of the present day are even more daring in their praise and admiration of Jesus.

Orthodox rabbis still cling to the traditional tales, but at least they are more cautious in the use of their language; there is no longer the reviling, vilifying and derisive vocabulary of olden times.

Many Jewish authors, both in Hebrew and in Yiddish, demanded a revision of the trial of Jesus. Some years ago one of the greatest Jewish writers, Dr. Chain Zhitlowsky, demanded a revision of the trial of Jesus. In *Das Neue Leben,* his journal, he says: "The Jewish legend concerning Jesus is a shameless blasphemy of all that should be considered holy and precious. . . . Every Jew should be proud of the fact that Jesus is our brother, flesh of our flesh and blood of our blood. We desire to put him back where he belongs."

Many Jewish novelists had Jesus as the "hero" of their novels. Outstanding among them, was the late *Shalom Ash,* who is generally considered as the greatest of Jewish novelists. His so-called "Christian" novels, such as *The Nazarene,* have raised a storm of protest from many notable Jews, especially in America. Nevertheless, they were translated into Hebrew and printed in Israel, and found a wide circulation there. Not only because his books are real masterpieces in literature, did the Jews in Israel eagerly read them, but also because there in the reborn homeland the Jews want to be free from all encumbrances and impediments which have thus far kept them away from the Truth, the free unadulterated truth which some of their leaders so badly distorted.

Many are asking themselves: "For nineteen hundred years we blindly followed our leaders. Now it has been proven beyond refutation that their whole account of Jesus is utter nonsense. Can we now trust the rabbis? May not the Christian's account be the right one? Have not our forefathers erred in their condemnation of Jesus?"

It is in Israel where a new day is dawning, the day when finally they will fully recognize Him whom they pierced, the day when they will shout: "Blessed is He who comes in the name of the Jehovah."

CHAPTER XV

SOME PRACTICAL WAYS OF APPROACH

Remember that bearing God's message to men has always been a difficult, thankless and risky task. We are not surprised that the great prophets, Moses, Amos, Jeremiah, Jonah, etc., tried hard to evade this task, but the Lord compelled them to do His will.

The Jews, surely, would not appreciate your telling them that the most important things which they have always believed to be right and good are wrong and unacceptable. No one would. But as Christ's ambassador you may expect no better fate than was His and should not expect immediate successes.

You bear the message whether they will hear it or not. But, as did the Master, bear it in love, with patience and tact.

Now let me suggest a few practical hints as to how you might make the first contact with the Jew.

Always be tactful. Don't show any condescension of superiority over him. He is sure that he is a member of the chosen people, a scion of kings and prophets, that his way of life, his culture, his religion is the best in the world. Don't try to controvert, to minimize these opinions. On the contrary, show him that you have high regard for his opinions, that as a student of the Bible you know his exalted position as one of a people chosen of God and that you hold sacred the words of his ancient prophets. Show him that you are aware of the lofty, noble qualities of the Jewish people, and that you admire them. Show him that you think it an unpardonable sin the Gentiles have committed in persecuting the Jewish people. Show him that you believe that his people are still to play a most important role in the history of mankind.

In short, without overdoing it, show Him love, kindness, readiness to help in any good way. You will later, when you have found a path to his heart, have an opportunity to show him that even he, as a Jew, is not infallible, even his people have been capable of sin and according to his own Bible, have often sinned. Their own prophets have rebuked and reproved them most sternly. According to their own Bible, God has often chastised His people severely but for the sake of their saintly forefathers and the everlasting covenant and their appointed mission, He did not destroy them utterly, as He destroyed other peoples in retribution for their iniquities.

Later on, when you find him attentive, you may remark cautiously, that those Jewish leaders who delivered Jesus into the hands of the Roman executioners, might have erred in condemning Him. Indeed, that is the opinion generally held by all, including a great many Jewish intellectuals, who know the story of Jesus and His environment.

Those leaders who rejected Jesus' claims and caused His death, were not of the best Jewish type. Indeed, their actions were very *un-Jewish* in their dealings with Jesus. The best that can be said in their exoneration is that they did it out of fear of the Romans, who might have used the new Messianic movements as an excuse for further and harsher oppression. Many Jewish writers have expressed such an opinion.

This is perhaps the best method to use in carrying out the initial steps. If you have succeeded in arousing his attention so that as he is ready to ask questions, to argue — then half the battle is won. All you have to do now is answer his questions honestly, reason with him (he may be earnest in his arguments, he may be cynical) and refute his mis-statements, his traditional misconceptions and purposeful falsehoods.

You have disarmed him, you have won half the battle, but you have not yet turned your opponent into a friend. You have not yet won him to Christ. But this task of regeneration, conversion, is not yours. It is only the Lord Himself who can work this miracle of grace. You may keep on praying for his salvation, you may help him, guide him faithfully, patiently on the way leading toward God's grace. And this you will do.

All I have said now depends on your having succeeded in rousing his attention to your words. If you have not succeeded in this, then try, try again. If after several trials you have not yet succeeded, do not be discouraged, do not despair. You keep on performing your duty to preach the Gospel. Victory is not your duty. The Lord will see to it if He wills so. Further on we shall present some of the typically Jewish questions and arguments about Christ and Christianity with suitable answers.

Let us now consider a few of the usual ways of making contact.

Approach the Jew like an adroit salesman, as if you have something to sell him at a great profit to both of you, which in your case is quite true. Think first how a good salesman would handle such a case. You may start with something casual, depending on the time and the place of meeting: on the bus, in a waiting room, in the park, on the play ground, at work, in the store, etc. A cursory starting point is the weather, some remarkable event of current interest, or you may even at once introduce yourself: "I am a Christian and have special tracts for Jews. I hope I don't offend by offering you some of them," or something like that. Of course, your next action depends on his reaction to your introductory remarks.

Other good approaches might be a recent crime wave, or some road fatalities, some catastrophe (flood, fire, etc.), some political event that had at that time aroused public attention. You may ask him about a hotel which he would recommend to you, or what is his opinion about some sports event. He most probably will respond and express his opinions. Then you find a fitting verse in the Bible that would illustrate or affirm your opinion (or his), or say: "If people only heeded God's words . . ." You will, thus, soon find out whether he wants to keep up the conversation.

Suppose you notice that your vis-a-vis on the bus, train, etc., is reading a paper or book in Hebrew characters. You start: "Excuse me . . . isn't that Hebrew you are reading? How I wish I could read the Bible in its original language. I am sure it is more beautiful and meaningful than in its translation." By his reaction to your introductory remarks, you would know how to continue the conversation. Start a discussion about the Bible as the greatest Book in the world, about its prophecies which are now being fulfilled. You may lead up to asking why the Jews refrain from reading the New Testament: "Is it not a Jewish book? A good book, of which the Jewish people have a right to be proud?" When you separate, you may declare your friendship for him, giving him your address and asking for his — so that correspondence may continue on the subject.

*   *   *   *   *

An occasion for contact may occur in any office, any place of business: "Aren't you Jewish?" Some Jews might think you are being sarcastic or offensive, so explain yourself: "I like to study faces. In the Jewish face I recognize an ancient aristocracy: especially the Jewish eyes. I find them so thoughtful, so gentle, so spiritual. Whenever I see a Jew I like to think of the face of Moses, Jesus and His followers. They must have looked like that. That may not sound as a compliment to many Jews who dislike Jesus, but I mean it as a compliment."

* * * * *

Suppose you have found out that your new neighbor is a Jew. Let him know by telephone, letter or orally that you are glad to have him as a neighbor; that you would appreciate making a more intimate acquaintance, visiting each other, etc. There are good chances that your family (man, wife, children) and his will become friends, or at least, pleasant neighbors, and be ready to meet and exchange opinions and views.

* * * * *

Invite your Jewish neighbors and friends on certain celebrations, such as birthdays, weddings or some religious occasions (for example, Christmas) or to some excursion or picnic, or even to some service or social in your church. Whether he accepts your invitation, or excuses himself for not accepting, you have the opportunity to continue your contact.

* * * * *

You may ask your Jewish friend to invite you to a service in the synagogue. If he agrees and takes you along to the synagogue, then you may get a stock of subjects for further contact and discussions that will last you for a long time and lead to the ultimate aim of his hearing the Gospel and accepting it. Of course he may find some pretext for refusing your request. In that case, too, you are afforded chances to make him hear your views. You may ask him why he refuses. His answers may complicate him so that you will have to extricate him from his perplexities.

* * * * *

A chance subject for contact with your Jewish grocer, attorney, bank-clerk, agent, peddler, etc., may be thus: "Oh, I'm so happy to see you today. I have some questions, and you being a Jew will probably know the proper answer. I had an argument with a friend about this — " Then you may ask: "What is the meaning of that 'amulet' which is fastened to the door posts of Jewish homes? What are phylacteries? What is the real meaning of 'Mashiach'? Why is the Israeli parliament called K'nesseth? What is the meaning of Sanhedrin?" and such like. It may turn out that he knows little or nothing about these things; in any case, you have subject matter for further contact.

Another excellent approach to the Jew may be made by mail. Send him a certain tract, the New Testament, or only a part of it. At about the same time you let him know by telephone or letter, or orally, that you sent it to him because you thought it might interest him, and that you would appreciate it if he would let you know his opinion about it. If he replies, keep up the contact in accordance with his reply. If after a certain time you get no reply ask him the reason for his silence. (Hasn't he read it yet? Has he had time to form an opinion? Has he not received it?) He may tell you that he is not interested in such things, and demand you stop sending any such "stuff." In that case write him that you did not intend any offense and that you hope he or she might still reconsider the matter and get interested, and that you are ever ready to be of help.

Preaching by mail does not have to be applied only to Jews whom you know. You may pick out, at random, names from the telephone book and contact them.

*   *   *   *   *

After some practical experience in this work you may find other effective ways of reaching the heart of the Jew. You may adopt some of the methods of the professional missionary, such as house-to-house visits, placing suitable literature in mail boxes, open air preaching in Jewish neighborhoods, etc.

Now, in your dealing with a Jew you should know what type of Jew he is, for there are various types, and the methods that are best for one may not be suitable to another. (See Chapter on "Types and Segments.")

CHAPTER XVI

OBJECTIONS AND QUESTIONS THE AVERAGE JEW IS LIKELY TO ASK

In your work among the Jews you are likely to encounter many obstacles and impediments, bitter contentions, arguments, belligerent controversy.

I assume that you are blessed with the love and the patience needed for this kind of work, but you probably lack the knowledge of what particular questions the Jew may ask you, and what you ought to answer.

A. SOME OF THE USUAL OBJECTIONS THE OBSERVANT OR ORTHODOX JEW MAY MENTION

Objection 1.

I have my own religion. I don't want any other.

Reply 1.

I don't intend to tell you of another religion. It is about your own religion, which is also mine, that I want to speak to you.

(Here he may cut you short: telling you he does not want to discuss it with a missionary, especially a Gentile. In that case you need extra tact and wisdom to retain his attention. He may tolerate or even encourage further discussion. Then, you may tell him that the Christian God is the Jewish God, that the Christian Messiah is the Jewish Messiah, that the Christian Bible is the Jewish Bible — the only difference is in the interpretation of it. And since the Christians are convinced that their interpretation is not only the true one, but also that on it depends life and death, they count it as their most sacred duty to bring this truth to all people including the Jews.)

Objection 2.

I know you worship three gods while we Jews have been taught from the days of our progenitor Abraham, on Sinai, and by our prophets and teachers that there is but One and only One God. This was, is and forever will be our faith. The Christians during the ages have tried their best, but unavailingly, to make us change our faith and you are not going to do it either.

Reply 2.

(Here you may tell him that true Christians respect and honor the Jewish people for their valiant and tenacious stand in their belief in the true God. Indeed, Christians feel much indebted to the Jews who taught them this faith in the one true God. Again it is the One God according to the Jewish conception of Him that Christians worship and none other.)

There are not three gods, but there are three aspects of Him, and this the Christians learned from the Jews, from the ancient Jews to whom the Bible was near and dear. It was only later on, in the Middle Ages, in order to counteract Christianity that some Jewish Rabbis began to teach that God has no attributes, that He cannot be imagined by man because He has no form, no appearance whatsoever. These Rabbis knew well that this sort of God is not the Jewish God, is not the God of the Bible. This was not the only distortion of the Bible which some Rabbis perpetrated in order to uphold a certain point of theirs.

Of course there is only One God, and He is so great that we puny creatures cannot comprehend Him with our puny minds. But does not the Bible, the Jewish Bible, from beginning to end, speak of God who often acts like a human being? He walks, He stands, He sits, He speaks, He is glad, He is angry. He comes in contact with man usually in the form of man. He dwelt in the Tabernacle in the wilderness. Later He dwelt in the Temple. He conversed with Abraham. He struggled with Jacob. He appeared before Joshua as a warrior. He also appeared in dreams and in visions, and by His spirit the Holy Ghost, He spoke to the prophets. It is hard to understand it but the Bible, the Jewish Bible, is full of God's threefold being: 1. The Incomprehensible "endless" Creator of all existence. 2. His revelation to man by assuming human form, so that mortals could grasp His presence. 3. His revelation through the Spirit.

In fact, God the Infinite, the Eternal, never asked man to believe in Him as an incomprehensible abstraction. One cannot believe in, or love, or pray to "something" which he cannot by any means comprehend or perceive. It is only the revealed God, the One who assumed human garb that the Jews, or any man, were asked to believe in, to love, to fear, to worship. He never spoke to the Jews as the inconceivable God, Creator of the universe, but, as *thy* God, the God of *your fathers*. On Sinai, in the greatest of

His revelations, His first words were, "I am *thy* God who have brought *thee* out of Egypt."

Objection 3.

Yes, but we believe that the same God — the abstract one who created the world — is also the concrete one who revealed Himself to man, whether in human form or by His spirit.

Reply 3.

Exactly so do we Christians believe. These *Three* are *One.* There is only that difference that you insist on emphasizing the word *One* as an absolute unity, while we prefer to emphasize the three-fold nature of the One.

Objection 4.

But the Bible tells us: "Hear ye, O Israel, Jehovah our God Jehovah is *One.*" This verse we repeat several times in the day — this is the most sacred principle of our faith, this is repeated by every Jew when he returns his soul to God.

This oneness precludes all plurality, all polytheism.

Reply 4.

(Here you have to explain to him that plurality is not polytheism.) Indeed, the Hebrew word which we translate *God* really is a plural noun. That very verse, most sacred to the Jews, if properly translated would be: ". . . Jehovah our God*s* . . ." The Bible starts with the words: "In the beginning God*s* created . . ." Further on we read, " — And God*s* said, let *us* make a man in *our* image — "

The plural noun for God is mostly defined by an adjective in the singular but sometimes also in the plural, which suggests or teaches that while God is One, He may appear in more than one form. Just as man consists of three different beings, body, soul and spirit; or for example, electricity, which no one really understands, may show itself as (1) light, (2) heat, (3) power. An "electric" train is driven by electricity, lighted by it, and in cold weather also is heated by it.

(The Ancient Rabbis, exegetes and exponents of the Bible well understood this plurality, or the threefold unity of God, as they expressed it in the Targums, Midrash, and the Kabbalist books. See special chapters on these subjects).

Objection 5.

If this plurality, or trinity as you call it, is the true nature of the Godhead, why does not the Bible speak of it in unequivocal words? Why only in hints, allusions and implications?

Reply 5.

It is because there was no need for telling things which were of common knowledge, of common thoughts and belief.

You may ask on what ground did RAMBAM (Maimonides) formulate the thirteen Articles of the Jewish Creed, which the Jews have to believe and recite in their morning prayer. There is no solid ground for them in the Bible except allusions. Like Christians, the Jews, too, believe in the Messiah because all the Bible is permeated with the "Coming of the Messiah." Like Christians the Jews, too, believe in the Resurrection.

The Bible nowhere says one must believe in any or all of these thirteen articles or principles, which RAMBAM enjoins every Jew to believe. What basis did he have for them?

Is it not because he knew that for hundreds of years this creed had been already the common belief of Judaism, and that up to his time there was no need of writing them down? It was only because in his time there was the danger of Jews going over to Christianity, or Mohammedanism or atheism that he found it necessary to define and formulate what the Jews must believe.

So also was the creed which is now known as "Christian." For many centuries, since Abraham, and even before, it was the common creed of all believers in God. There was no occasion for any of the authors of the Bible to record something that everyone knew. It was only after the people began to doubt, to waver, to form schisms, that some of the followers of Jesus, the Church fathers, had to formulate the creed, which was then in danger of being attacked, abandoned and forgotten.

There might have been another reason: In the times of Moses and the other prophets the Jews were still inclined to revert to idolatry, like the people around them. Thus the Biblical writers had to be very cautious in the choice of words. If Scripture had used the word *trinity*, it might have led someone to believe that it sanctions polytheism, whereas by the time of Christ this danger no longer existed. Then the threefold unity of the Godhead could be generally spoken of and so it became the common belief.

In short, there is nothing which the Christian believes that is not in the Bible and which the Jewish people believed for hundreds of years even after biblical times.

Objection 6.

Ridiculous, preposterous, blasphemy! Do you mean to say that all those fancy dogmas of Christianity are in accordance with Judaism? With the Jewish Bible?

How absurd all this talk about Jesus, that poor carpenter's son, asserting that he was the Messiah, that he was born of a virgin, that after he died he rose from the grave and went up to heaven. All that stuff you may believe, if you please, but don't tell me that it is in accord with our Bible.

Reply 6.

All this may sound absurd and contrary to human reasoning but it is certainly in harmony with your Bible. Jesus was and is the Messiah because all the prophecies of the Bible about the Messiah were fulfilled in Him. These include His virgin birth and all the other things which you consider so absurd.[1]

True, these are irrational, unfathomable mysteries, but so is all life, all existence. We are surrounded by millions of inexplicable mysteries. At any rate these "absurdities" are the very essence of the Bible.

Why is it easier for the modern Jew, remote from Bible teaching, to fathom God appearing in human form (as to Abraham, Jacob, Joshua, Manoah) for a short time, than to believe that He appeared in human form for a longer time — as in Jesus?

Jews know, although they don't understand it, that God lived in the Holy of Holies, because the Bible says so. Surely the omnipresent God did not leave all the universe to take care of itself while He was sojourning with the Jews in the Tabernacle and later in the Temple.

But because the Bible says so, Jewish believers are sure it was so. They even have a word for it — the "Shechina" which implies, "God-living-among-men."

Thus, too, the Bible speaks of the Messiah as a divine person, incarnation of the Infinite, Son of God.

When the Bible foretells the Messiah's birth of a virgin, why not believe this miracle as any other miracle recorded in the Bible? Is not every birth a miracle?

Death, too, is a miracle, and rising from death is a miracle. The whole Bible from beginning to end is a record of miracles, so when you do believe part of it, why not all?

These records, these doctrines about the Messiah are not the creations, fabrications of Gentiles. The Christians learned them from Jewish teachers and preachers. Many rabbis, especially the mystics *(Kabbalists)*, were teaching and expounding these doctrines long after certain Jewish authorities discredited such teachings for

[1] See chapter on "Christianity Is Completed Judaism."

argument's sake. Indeed, they are *Jewish* doctrines; purely Jewish precepts.

Objection 7.

We Jews could not accept Christianity, as it is full of superstitions, and doctrines which are repugnant to Jewish taste, sentiment, ideas and principles; such as original sin, vicarious atonement (by Messiah), mediation and the like. We cannot believe that people now, thousands of years after Adam, should be punished for his sin. We cannot believe that one man can atone for the sins of another man. We have a straight, direct access to God and we don't need anyone, no Messiah, no Son of God, to mediate, to intercede between us and God.

Reply 7.

Original Sin — These ideas which you now express, are those of some liberal Jews. They are not according to the Bible, not even according to traditional Judaism. According to the Bible and to post-biblical Judaism, suffering and death came to mankind because of Adam's sin. Because of the voluntary suffering and death (the supreme sacrifices) offered by another man, the greatest of men, the Messiah, death was abolished, lost its sting. (See Appendix.)

Mediation — Mediation is an old Hebrew principle, as old as Melchizedek, priest of the Most High God, and Abraham, who interceded for Abimelech (Genesis 20:7, 17) and for Sodom (Genesis 18:23-32). Moses and other men of God interceded for their people. The priests were mainly mediators and intercessors between sinful man and a Holy God. The people and kings begged the prophets to intercede for them before God.

Throughout the ages, Jews were accustomed to beg saintly men to intercede. They traveled long and hazardous distances to rabbis or to the graves of saintly people to seek their intercessions. In cases of troubles (sickness, etc.), people hastened to the graves of relatives to supplicate that they might appear before the Throne of Mercy and intercede for help. People have been hired to say *Kaddish,* and learn *Mishnaoth* in order that the departed relatives may have peace in the other world.

Among the most solemn prayers of New Year's Day certain angels are pleaded with to bring the prayers before the Throne of Glory. In one of those prayers even YESHUA SAR HAPANIM, which may mean Jesus, "Lord of the Innermost," or, "Lord of the Face," is implored to mediate between the Jewish people and God. As to how this Jesus got into the prayer book, no one has yet found a good explanation. Nor does any Jew know to whom this great Mediator refers. In most new editions of the prayer book, for the High Holy days, this prayer is omitted.

At any rate, mediation is a (good) Jewish doctrine and Christianity obtained it from Judaism.

Objection 8.

All right. But all this talk of a Mediator is superfluous. Since you claim that Christianity is all taken from Judaism of old, and thus, by your religion (conviction) you are a real Jew, why not preach to us to be good Jews, to keep all the Law, and not to sin, so we shall not need any intercession, any forgiveness? No sin — no punishment, no expiation.

Reply 8.

That would be fine, if it could be achieved. Think of Adam and Eve; they had everything any creature could desire. All that God wanted from them was just a little obedience: All paradise was at their disposal except one tree, whose fruit they were not to eat. Had they obeyed God, this world would have remained a paradise to mankind, but they didn't and they and their offspring were cursed for it.

Later, God chose unto Himself a people that would in course of time become a blessing to accursed mankind. Till that glorious time came He gave them a set of laws by which they would be disciplined, educated and kept holy. Every earthly blessing was promised to those who would submit to God's grace and obey His commandments, and a curse was laid (or rather the original curse remained intact) upon the one who would disobey Him. Yet, if the sinner repented and offered a certain prescribed sacrifice (as a symbol that he himself is worthy of death) his sin was forgiven, or "covered," as the Hebrew means.

Were the Jewish people, the chosen people, better than Adam and Eve? They certainly were not. After God had brought them out from Egypt by so many marvels, after they had heard His voice on Sinai, accompanied by wondrous visions, after they solemnly swore to obey the *One God, their God,* the God who brought them out of Egypt, after all these they went and made themselves a golden calf, and worshiped it as *their god.*

Disobedience, rebellion against God, was committed repeatedly by individuals as well as by the people as a whole, so the Bible tells us. But then, there were the sacrifices for individual as well as for national expiation.

Now there is no Jew who keeps all the laws of God; what can he do to be forgiven since there is no sacrifice to be offered in expiation of his sin?

Objection 9.

We hope and pray that God would bring us back to our "promised land," there we shall reinstitute the sacrifices as prescribed by Moses. Till that time we offer prayer instead of sacrifice. If a Jew sins he may atone by repentance, prayer and charity, and for these we need no mediator: also the Day of Atonement is set for the atonement of our sins.

Reply 9.

The Rabbis so taught you, but the Bible expressly says that there is *no* remission of sin without blood (Genesis 4:1-4; Leviticus 17:11).

If prayer and fasting, almsgiving and repentance were effective for atonement, why do the Jewish people still feel guilty? Why are they not forgiven? Why do they still have to suffer for their sins? There is not in the whole world a people who repents more, prays more, is more charitable. Why does not the Merciful God, the God of Israel, accept all these signs of submission and penitence?

The great prophets, beginning with Moses, have warned their people that if they disobeyed God's Word they would be exiled from their country and then, in their exile if they truly, wholeheartedly repent He would return them to their country. The first part of the prophecy was fulfilled — they rebelled against God, and they were exiled. The second part has not yet been fulfilled.[2] Why? All through exile in diaspora the people prayed God for forgiveness, prayed for the Messiah, prayed for the return to the Promised Land, prayed for the reinstitution of the holy altar and the sacrifices. They performed all the rites and meticulously, punctiliously kept all the laws — which the rabbis taught them to keep and perform in order to find favor in the eyes of God. But all to no avail.

Why, O why! Why was not their unparalleled suffering

[2] Only a small number of "Jews" (as they were after called) returned from Babylonian exile and only for a short period were they really an independent sovereign nation. After (the rejection of Christ and) the destruction of Jerusalem the Jews were dispersed to all corners of the earth. The rise of the new Jewish State — the State of Israel — again like the return from Babylon, is only a partial return, since the greatest part of the people are still in exile.

throughout their exile, why were not all their good deeds enough to atone for their sins? Is not God, their God — the God of love and mercy and forgiveness?

Can there be another answer than that only sacrificial blood has had the power to atone? Since the sacrifices of animals have ceased, and since they have rejected the supreme sacrifice of the Messiah, there can be nothing else to atone for sin.

Another question might be asked of the Jews (remember we deal now with *observant* Orthodox Jews): They continuously, in prayer, confess their sins for which they have been exiled; on the High Holidays they recite long lists of sins "for which *we* were exiled from *our* land." These lists are being recited and confessed several times on the Day of Atonement — the *Day* on which, according to the Jewish faith, God forgives their sins. Does He forgive them? Judging from what has been meted out to the Jews all through their exile, and their still being in hostile exile, it seems that He rejects their confession and their repentance.

Why, oh why?

There can only be one answer: Among the long list of sins and crimes which they confess to have committed, many of which they did not, many they could not have committed, they have been leaving out one sin, the greatest sin: their rejection of the Messiah — Jesus. When their leaders delivered Him into the hands of the Romans to do away with Him as a criminal, the Jewish people, as a whole, acquiesced. Since then, the people, as a whole, justify the judgment of their forefathers and He is still rejected by the people. Isn't this *the* sin for which the Jews do not ask for pardon, and for which they are still unpardoned? If this is not the sin for which they have been suffering, for which they have been castigated during the last nineteen centuries, what else is?

Objection 10.

Let us not argue about the supernatural. Let us get down to facts, to life. The Messiah whom we Jews expected was to be a mighty King who would initiate and institute a new world-order of peace and justice in which the nations of all the world would be guided by the people of Israel — out of Zion. But Jesus did none of these. Wars are being waged now no less than before. There is no more justice now than there was before, and as to the Jewish people, not only had he not helped them but could not even help Himself when he was arrested and executed as a criminal. Moreover, the most horrible crimes against the Jews have been perpetrated in His name.

Reply 10.

(You may tell him that he unintentionally raised a serious problem, that age-old problem of man's free will and God's foreknowledge, or predestination.) Ancient sages (both Jews and Gentiles) tried in vain to solve it, and we moderns are no better off in this respect. God certainly is omniscient and prescient, and of course He knows that a certain man, or men, will commit a certain sin at a certain time. In such case, one may ask, has that particular man, or men, any choice not to commit that sin?

He must have that choice. All religions teach that man has a free will, otherwise he would be an automaton and not responsible for his deeds. On the other hand, should that man decide not to commit that sin then something is amiss with God's prescience.

As has been said, it is an old enigma and man will perhaps never be able to solve it properly.

Had the Jewish people, as a whole, hailed Jesus as the Messiah the world would obviously have changed entirely. The Messianic Age of peace and happiness, as Isaiah foresaw it, might have been a fact. But they rejected Him and the age of "Days of the Messiah" as the Jews call it, has been postponed. The Jewish nation as a whole had sinned, so consequently the nation as a whole was punished by the postponement of its redemption, of its being elevated to a Holy Nation, a kingdom of Priests, and teachers and guides or rulers of all the world. If the whole people had accepted Jesus as the Messiah, then truly within a short time they would have brought the message of the Messiah to all the world and all war and sorrow and pain would have vanished. But since only individual Jews accepted Him and they in turn went out into all the world and won only individuals to the Messiah, while the nations as a whole remained in ignorance of God and His Torah, it is no wonder that there still exist injustice, war and sorrow.

The prophets foresaw all this. They saw that the Messiah would be rejected, persecuted and killed as an expiation for the sin of man. They also foresaw His coming again as the great ruler of the universe, who will abolish death forever and endow redeemed man with a life of bliss forever.

The wise rabbis knew of these two appearances of the Messiah and they named the first "Mashiach ben Yosef" (Messiah, son of Joseph) who was destined to suffering and death and the other "Machiach ben David" (Son of David) who is to appear in glory and fulfill all law and prophecy and inaugurate "The World to Come." (See chapter on "The Messiah.")

There is still much confusion among the less informed Jews as regards the two appearances of the Messiah. They know little of the suffering Messiah. (To these you may point out the passages in the Bible — Psalm 22, Daniel 9:24-27; Isaiah 53, etc.)

It surely is surprising to see how much space the Bible devotes to the suffering and dying Messiah for the sins of mankind, with the space it devotes to the finally triumphant Messiah.

Some rabbis, (usually) antagonistic to Christianity, interpret those passages as referring to the suffering Jewish people, but any scrutiny of the text will at once show that it cannot mean the Jews. For example: Isaiah 53:8 last clause.

In reply to the charge that Christianity has been the greatest enemy of the Jews; that the vilest, cruelest atrocities were perpetrated in Jesus' name against the Jews, may I state briefly: whoever does wrong, or harm to anyone, especially to the Jews, is not a true Christian. Because true Christianity means to follow Christ, which implies to love, to sacrifice, to forgive. How much sin and crime has been committed in the name of God! Those so-called Christians who persecuted the Jews had not and could not cite anything that Jesus said or did, that would support their evil deed. But they could cite (and they did so) many passages in the Hebrew "Tanach" (Old Testament) where God, the God of Israel, rebuked and reproved the Jewish people in most severe terms and visited upon them the most severe chastisement. Should God be rejected because some fools took His name in vain? because some perverted mind had abused His name? Why, then, should Jews blame Jesus for the misdeeds of beguiled, misled or benighted people?

Since the Pharaohs of Egypt, long before the advent of Christianity, and through the ages, the Jews have been persecuted. Even from the simple human standpoint it can be easily understood. People do not like strangers, and because the Jews are the most strange, the most peculiar, they are the least liked. Wherever Jews lived they were disliked, distrusted. All races, nations, religions, sects, parties, all social strata (rich, poor, aristocrats, commoners, capitalists, socialists), all have had some grudge against the Jews.

The main reason for this dislike is, surely, the Jewish way of keeping aloof, or at least keeping to themselves. However, this dislike is not particularly a "Christian" fault or shortcoming. On the contrary, only in "Christian" countries did the Jews survive; only there did they prosper; only there have they acquired rights and privileges equal, or almost equal, to those of the other, the native inhabitants. Once in a while, the evil spirit prevailed and it came to bitter persecution and violence even in so-called Christian countries, but there it was only a passing madness, while in non-Christian countries, the passionate anti-Jewish outbreaks brought total annihilation. The more a country was influenced by the spirit and love of Christ, the better it was for the Jews to live there. Modern anti-Semitism which climaxed in Nazism and Communism is only the result of the decline of Christianity among these people.

An Anti-Semite is not and cannot be a Christian, because he has to hate the founder, the propagators, the first churches, because they all were true faithful Jews, and because Christianity is all based on the Jewish Bible, a book that the Christian is to use as the standard of life.

Look around and you will see that the only friends the Jewish people have now are Christians. Only Christian nations helped in the establishment of the new state of Israel; only Christian nations are helping its survival in the midst of implacable enemies.

So the notion that Christianity is the greatest foe of the Jews is a base lie invented by misleading and misled leaders.

But whatever human beings do to the Jews or to anyone else has nothing to do with the saving grace of Christ, and this is our message.

B. Some (of the Usual) Objections of the Liberal Jews

"Liberal" Jews (Reformists, Conservatives and others) usually contend that Christianity with its irrational doctrines cannot be accepted by the Jewish people, because for thousands of years, they have been taught a simple, logical and rational religion. All those dogmas, of the Trinity, God becoming Man, Virgin Birth, the Fall of Man, Original Sin, Christ's Vicarious Atonement, Hell with its horrors, etc., are contradictory to reason and to the spirit of Judaism.

Such objections are often used in religious controversy by Jews who are "very proud" of their "Judaism" which they either disbelieve or of which they are quite ignorant.

Some half-baked scholars "prove" that the Christian dogmas were introduced from pagan mythology.

To such Jews you may reply: "Whether these dogmas are irrational, or are of pagan origin, is a different question. But, whatever they are, they are truly Jewish. Christianity acquired them from Jews, from the Jewish Bible, from Jewish belief, and from Jewish teachers."

If what is irrational (to our minds) is what repels Jews from Christianity then they ought to repudiate their own Bible, their own Talmud and all their religious literature. The most revered part of the Bible, the "Five Books of Moses," is from beginning to end a succession of things (stories and laws) which could be called unreasonable. Many scoffers, some of them known as "great men," had little respect and much ridicule for these five books. And if this is so, what is left of Judaism, of which they are so proud? Moreover, just as Jewish scholars find pagan origin to some Christian doctrines and practices, so have other Gentile scholars found pagan origin to Jewish beliefs and practices such as circumcision, sacrifices, and various other laws. So, you may tell them, we are in the same boat. You can't deny the one without denying the other.

On the other hand, no part of the Bible, whether of the Old Testament or New Testament, may be discredited because it contains something that had already been written or done before by other people. One must remember, that, if the Infinite God revealed Himself to man, then He had to appear to him in a manner as to be understood by him. If man of antiquity was accustomed to mutilate his body, to offer sacrifices and the like, when he wanted to pay homage, to appease his god, if that was man's way, if that was how man understood it, the Lord in His infinite mercy and love for man dealt with him in his own way. Only He taught him to limit his practices to more "humane" ways, forbidding harmful mutilations and human sacrifice, etc. At the same time He let them know, by His Spirit through the prophets, that there would come a time when circumcision of the "heart" would replace that of the flesh, when the "supreme sacrifice" would do away with all other sacrifice, when everyone would *know the law* and would know what the Lord wants him to do in each case. He will not have to ask anyone else, rabbi or priest, what to do.

Some Gentile scholars, with a touch of Anti-Semitism and atheism, have often disparaged Judaism by showing the Code of Hammurabi as proof that the Jews were not the first to have a written law. Well, what of it? Any sensible man may know that wherever there was an organized society where people lived together, they must have had rules and regulations as to how to make life more endurable and more pleasant.

Space does not permit enlargement here upon this subject and it is also irrelevant when dealing with the Jew. You may use this only as an example in regard to some Jewish arguments, that all the nice sayings of Jesus, parables, etc., were taken from the Jews. To prove this they quote certain passages from the Talmud, showing that the rabbis had *already* said that.

In reply say: "As Jesus was a Jew, who always lived among Jews, and was reared in Jewish tradition, and who knew the Torah, He must have been speaking in the Jewish manner; but most of His sayings were unique and new, and the people marveled hearing Him speak as no one 'spoke like it before.' Surely He did not copy His sayings from the Talmud which was written hundreds of years after Him.

"True, there are some things in both the Old Testament and New Testament which seem unnatural, unreasonable; well, there are millions of things around us that we cannot understand. Some of them we may get to know, and some, never. All life is a fathomless mystery. Rising from death is unusual, unnatural, but it is no more of a mystery than death itself, than birth itself. Being born from a virgin is unnatural, but any birth is beyond our understanding. It is only that we have become accustomed to this mystery. And so it is with the other miracles and mysteries of the Bible. We may only say that God knows what He is doing and that His will must be done."

The liberal's view about sin and retribution is extremely vague. There is *no* national sin, they say, and God did not disperse the Jews from their country on account of some sin, but sent them out into the world to spread Judaism among the Gentiles. They don't say how the Jews fulfilled this mission. However, this view is entirely different from Judaism. Not only does the Bible often refer to the national sins and threat of retribution by expulsion from their land and dispersion among the nations, but it also opposes the general Jewish conception of this subject. The Jews often repeatedly confess in their prayers that "because of *our sins* were we exiled from *our land*," several times daily they pray that God may have mercy, for His own· sake and for the sake of their patriarchs, to bring them back to their land, where they might atone for their sins with sacrifices as prescribed of old.

At any rate, let him explain to you how God deals with sinners — what would prevent men from sinning?

One of the objections of liberal Jews against the Christian faith is that it requires bloody atonement, that a man had to die for the sins of others. Also, that it speaks of eternal punishment, of "gnashing of teeth" and the like. These liberals contend that God cannot be "so bad" as to allow human suffering on account of some frailty. These good people seem to have a sugar-coated God, who would do only the things which according to them are sweet and good and harmless.

In that case they might as well reject all Judaism because it, or rather the Old Testament speaks of God, not only as the Merciful, the Compassionate, the forgiving, but also the *"jealous God, visiting the iniquity of the fathers upon the children."* So God Himself introduced Himself to the Jewish people in His Ten Commandments on Sinai (see Exodus 20:5, 6). Indeed, liberal Gentiles have condemned the Old Testament because of its "cruel" God. Why cannot these good people understand that like a good surgeon, God has sometimes to administer some bitter remedy, or even to amputate a part of the body in order to preserve the remainder? If these liberals believe in that very liberal Supreme Being as they claim, why does He (or *It* allow so much suffering in the world? Why sickness, earthquakes, floods, droughts, etc.?

Should we puny mortals ask our Creator why He does this, and why not otherwise? Can we not understand that He knows better what is good and what not? In this the Orthodox Jew is more correct when he declares: "All that the Compassionate does He does it for the good" (or "is good"). Or on hearing bad news of the death of a relative, etc., he is to exclaim: "God had given, God has taken: *Blessed be the True Judge.*"

The liberal Jew is ready to concede that Jesus was a great man, some go even as far as to admit that He was the greatest Jew that ever lived, but no further. He was a man, but no more than that.

To these we may say, if Jesus was great, righteous, just and honest, as those liberals admit, then we must believe His words, when He claimed to be the Son of God, the Messiah (etc.). If what He claimed to be was false, illusory, misleading, then He was not a good, just, and truthful man. He was the reverse of all that.

Some of the liberal's objections are like those of the Orthodox (in regard to "mediation," for example, which we have already discussed).

C. Dealing With Agnostics (Etc.)

It is much easier to deal with Jewish agnostics and atheists than with non-Jewish ones, because, no matter how vociferously he claims disbelief, by the fact that he. is of Jewish descent he *is* religious to some degree. No matter how much he denies his Jew-ishness, he is partial to Jews and Judaism. Why? Because in every Jew's heart there is a latent spark, which was once kindled by the ancient prophets and fed and kept alive for long ages. Every Jew is a potential minister of God. This latent spark you may kindle to a flame, giving out light and warmth.

Ask him to explain the unparalleled enigma of history — the existence (perpetuation) of his people after centuries of perse-cution, oppression and massacre. No other people in the whole wide world, could have survived such catastrophes as have be-fallen the Jewish people. All efforts of mighty people to destroy them, to extirpate them, were of no avail. Can this fact, this phenomenon be explained otherwise than that an almighty super-natural power has been keeping and guiding this peculiar people, and that this "power" has done it for some purpose? Can he, or anyone, explain why the Bible written by different authors in dif-ferent ages, mostly by primitive man and, to modern standards, also ignorant, has become the world's best, most beloved, most read book, and that in spite of all attacks against it? Is this not due to its divine inspiration and the divine will that it should be intact, studied and obeyed?

Of course you may also use the same evidence of the existence of a personal God, as may be used in argument with Gentile athe-ists, etc.

You may sometimes hear a cynical Jew say: "You want me to believe in the Son, when I don't believe in the Father," or, "I don't believe in the existence of the Father, how can I believe in the Son?" Jesus must have been aware of such people when He argued with His persecutors (see John 5:19-47), "For had ye be-lieved Moses, you would have believed me: for he wrote of me. But if ye believe not his writings, how shall ye believe my words?"

Chapter XVII

HOW TO IDENTIFY THE MESSIAH[1]

(The final argument with the average Jew, especially the one who has some leaning toward tradition and ancient Jewish culture)

I. What More Could Jesus Have Done Than He Did to Persuade the High Priests and the Other Leaders That He Was the True Messiah?

It was the time when the Messiah was anxiously expected. "And she coming in that instant gave thanks likewise unto the Lord, and spake of him to all them that looked for redemption in Jerusalem" (Luke 2:38); "And as the people were in expectation, and all men mused in their hearts of John, whether he were the Christ, or not" (Luke 3:15); "When the men were come unto him, they said, John Baptist hath sent us unto thee, saying, Art thou he that should come? or look we for another?" (Luke 7:20). Hard-pressed by the cruel Roman conquerors; split among themselves into contending sects; with a perplexed confused leadership; the people as a whole were as scattered, straying sheep, waiting for the true shepherd to lead them unto green pastures; waiting for a sign from God that He had not forsaken them, waiting for a new revelation, a new message, waiting for comfort, for love. They knew that the time was ripe for the Redeemer to come; Daniel, the "*greatly* beloved" (Daniel 10:10-12), had foretold the fixed time for it. There was a rumbling also in the heathen world. There, too, it was felt that something somewhere was going to happen, that a divine person was about to appear and save the world.

At that momentous time Jesus came. John (the Elijah who was to precede the Messiah) witnessed to the people that followed him, that this Jesus was the Messiah. Jesus Himself claimed to be the Messiah; His deeds, His whole life affirmed that He was

[1] See chapter on "The Messiah."

the Messiah. All the prophecies of the Torah pointed out that He was the Messiah. The people felt that He was the Messiah, the expected Comforter, the Redeemer.

There was opposition only from one side, from the cowardly, egotistic, blind "ruling" class. They may be compared to some of the chief priests such as those mentioned in II Chronicles 36: 14-16: "Moreover all the chief of the priests, and the people, transgressed very much after all the abominations of the heathen; and polluted the house of the Lord which he had hallowed in Jerusalem. And the Lord God of their fathers sent to them by his messengers, rising up betimes, and sending; because he had compassion on his people, and on his dwelling place: But they mocked the messengers of God, and despised his words, and misused his prophets, until the wrath of the Lord arose against his people, till there was no remedy"; or, those whom Isaiah had in mind when he lamented (Isaiah 3:12) ". . . O, my people, they which lead thee cause thee to err, and destroy the way of thy paths."

And these leaders succeeded in splitting and scattering the people even more than they were previously, they succeeded in driving them away from Jesus who *so* wanted to gather them into His fold: "O Jerusalem, Jerusalem, thou that killest the prophets, and stonest them which are sent unto thee, how often would I have gathered thy children together, even as a hen gathereth her chickens under her wings, and ye would not!" (Matthew 23:37).

Again, what could Jesus have done more than He did to make those leaders confess the truth of His Messiahship?

II. How Could the Messiah Be Identified Today by the Jews?

The Jewish people as a whole still expect the coming of the Messiah. The observant Jew still prays for His coming, and he daily declares his belief in His coming, very soon. Now suppose that somewhere (let us say in Jerusalem) a man known or unknown, suddenly appears and claims that he is the long expected Messiah. How could he prove his claim? By what could he be identified? By what could he prove that he is of the lineage of David? There is no Jewish family in the world now that could produce any legal document to show that he is the offspring of King David. Would miracles performed by him convince the leaders that he is the Messiah? Probably not.

Rambam (Maimonides) who formulated the credal statement of the Messiah and made it encumbent on every Jew to believe in it, asserted that there would be nothing supernatural about the Messiah's coming, that he would only redeem Israel from foreign yoke and establish peace. He does not say how the Messiah will achieve that without any supernatural means. However, unlike Rambam, who was a rationalist, the people believe that the Messiah will perform many great miracles in establishing the Messianic Age.

Now suppose he performs miracles. Would that cause the people to believe in him? He may win to his side the extreme Orthodox Jews of Jerusalem if he adapts himself to their ways, in which case the rest of the people would have nothing to do with him. If he would not agree to all their ways, they would declare that he works his miracles by the power of Satan, and they would reject him and endeavor to destroy him. Other people would say that he is only a trickster, or a magician. What else could he do to prove his Messiahship? What could he do to persuade the leaders to relinquish their government posts and let him rule over them?

Suppose they did let him rule, what next? What would he initiate? What new things would he introduce? How would the Jews in Israel and in Diaspora react? How would the Arab world react? etc.

I only want to show that the Jewish leaders of the present day would not recognize anyone who would now come and claim to be the expected Messiah, since he could not produce any more proof of his Messiahship than did Jesus before the high priests of old, but much less.

Now, to all the evidences that were before the people during Jesus' life on earth, there are added the evidences of His death and resurrection, the evidences of history, the evidences of hundreds of millions of people who have been acclaiming Jesus as the Messiah, although not all have been following in His footsteps. What more evidence could any person now bring forward to prove his Messiahship?

The only thing for the Jew to do is to read carefully the story of the life of Jesus as recorded in the New Testament, where he will see that not the leaders who condemned Him were right but that He of whom Moses and the Prophets wrote was in the right. Because Jesus, and He alone, can easily be identified as the One of whom they prophesied: the Messiah — Redeemer of mankind.

Here are some of the identification marks of the promised Messiah:

HE WAS TO BE
(According to Old Testament Prophecy):

THIS PROPHECY WAS FULFILLED IN JESUS
(According to the New Testament):

I. *The Seed of woman who would bruise Satan's head:*
"And I will put enmity between thee and the woman, and between thy seed and *her* seed; it shall bruise thy head, and thou shalt bruise his heel" (Gen. 3:15).

I. ". . . God sent forth His Son *made of a woman* . . . to redeem . . ." (Gal. 4:4).
". . . For this purpose the Son of God was manifested, that He might destroy the works of the devil" (I John 3:8).

II. *Of Abraham's Seed:*
"And I will establish my covenant between me and thee and thy *seed* . . ." (Gen. 17:7). See also Gen. 22:18; 21:12; 28:14; 12:1-3.

II. "Now to Abraham and his seed were the promises made. He saith not, And to seeds, as to many: but as of one, And to thy *seed*, which is Christ" (Gal. 3:16). See also John 11:51, 52 and Hebrews 11:17-19.

III. *Of the House of David:*
"I will set up thy *seed* and establish his kingdom for ever" (II Sam. 7:12, 13). See also Gen. 49:10; Ps. 132:11; 2:12; 89:3, 4; 110:1, 2; Isa. 11:1; Jer. 23:5; 33:17, 20, 21.

III. "Of David's *seed* hath God according to His promise raised unto Israel a Saviour, Jesus" (Acts 13:23). See also Acts 2:29, 30; Matt. 1:1; 22:42-45; Mark 11:9, 10; 12:35-37; Luke 1:31-33; Rom. 1:3, 4; Rev. 5:5; 22:16.

IV. *Preceded by a Messenger:*
"Behold, I will send my messenger; he shall prepare the way" (Mal. 3:1). See also Isa. 40:3.

IV. "He shall go before him to make ready a people for the Lord" (Luke 1:17). See also Matt. 3:1, 3.

V. *Born of a Virgin:*
"Behold, a virgin shall conceive, and bear a son, and shall call his name Immanuel" (Isa. 7:14).

V. "Now, . . . when his mother Mary was espoused to Joseph before they came together she was found with child of the Holy Ghost" (Matt. 1:18; see also Matt. 1:21-23).

VI. "Now, Jesus was born in Bethlehem of Judea" (Matt. 2:1).

VI. *Born in Bethlehem:*
"But thou *Bethlehem* Ephrata, though thou be little among the thousands of Judah, yet out of thee shall he come forth unto me that is to be ruler in Israel, whose goings forth have been from of old, from everlasting . . ." (Micah 5:2).

VII. "I am the good shepherd, and know my sheep and am known of mine" (John 10:11-16). See also John 10:27,28; Matt. 15:24; Mark 14:27; I Peter 2:25; Heb. 13:20.

VII. *The Shepherd:*
"He shall feed his flock like a *shepherd:* he shall gather the lambs with his arm, and carry them in his bosom, and shall gently lead those that are with young" (Isa. 40:11). See also Ps. 23:1-4; 80:1; Zech. 13:7; Ezek. 34:23, 24.

VIII. "And he shall send Jesus Christ, for Moses truly said, A *prophet* shall the Lord our God raise up like unto me" (Acts 3:20-22).

VIII. *The Prophet:*
"The Lord thy God will raise up unto thee a *prophet* like unto me: unto him ye shall hearken" (Deut. 18:15).

IX. "Thou art a priest for ever after the order of Melchizedek" (Heb. 5:5, 6). See also Heb. 4:14-16.

IX. *The Priest:*
"Thou art a priest for ever after the order of Melchizedek" (Ps. 110:4). See also Zech. 6:13.

X. ". . . Thou sayest that I am *King.* To this end was I born" (John 18:33, 37).
"The Lord God shall give unto him the throne of his father David" (Luke 1:32, 33). See also Matt. 28:18; John 1:49; Rev. 11:15.

X. *The King:*
"Rejoice greatly, O daughter of Zion: shout, O daughter of Jerusalem; behold thy *King* cometh unto thee: he is just and having salvation; lowly and riding upon an ass . . ." (Zech. 9:9). See also Ps. 2:6; Jer. 23:5, 6.

XI. "For unto you is born this day in the city of David a Saviour, which is Christ the Lord" (Luke 2:11). See also Matt. 1:21; Rom. 11:26; 11:27; John 3:14, 15; Acts 13:23; 4:12; Heb. 9:12; Gal. 4:4, 5; I Peter 1:18-21; Rev. 5:9.

XI. *The Redeemer:*
"And the *Redeemer* shall come unto Zion, and unto them that turn from transgression in Jacob, saith the Lord" (Isa. 59: 20). See also Isa. 19:20; 45:15; 44: 22, 23; 49:6-10; Hos. 1:7; Jer. 33:16.

XII. *The Sacrifice:*

All the passages in the Old Testament which predict the humiliation, suffering and death of the Messiah as the Sacrifice and atonement for the sins of mankind were exactly fulfilled in Jesus. Isaiah chapter 52 and particularly 53 give a clear picture of the promised Messiah: hated, despised, reviled, rejected, condemned and executed as a criminal — all this as a sacrifice to atone for the sins of the world. And all this was fulfilled in the ministry of Jesus to the minutest detail.

Let us have some comparison between the prediction in the Old Testament and the fulfillment in the New Testament:

IN THE OLD TESTAMENT

IN THE NEW TESTAMENT

Isaiah, Chapters 52 and 53 compare with *The Four Gospels*

A. *A Stranger:*
"I am become a stranger unto my brethren, and an alien unto my mother's children (Ps. 69: 8).

A. "He came unto his own and his own received him not" (John 1:11). Also John 7:3, 5.

B. *A Stumbling Stone:*
"A stone of stumbling and a rock of offence to both the houses of Israel" (Isa. 8:14).

B. "They stumbled at that stumbling stone. As it is written, Behold I lay in Zion a stumbling-stone and rock of offence: and whosoever believeth on him shall not be ashamed" (Rom. 9:32, 33).

C. *Hated:*
"Thus saith the Lord, the Redeemer of Israel and his Holy One, to him whom man despiseth" (Isa. 49:7). Also Ps. 69:4; 2:1, 2.

C. ". . . but now have they both seen and hated both me and my Father . . . the word written in their law. They hated me without a cause" (John 15:24, 25). Also Acts 4:27.

D. *Reproached:*
"The reproaches of them that reproached thee are fallen upon me" (Ps. 69:9).

D. "For even Christ pleased not himself, but as it is written, The reproaches of them that reproached thee fell on me" (Rom. 15:3).

E. *Mocked:*
"All they that see me laugh me to scorn, they shoot out the lip, they shake the head, saying, He trusted on the Lord that he would deliver him, seeing he delighted in him" (Ps. 22:7, 8).

E. "They that passed by reviled him, wagging their heads . . . Likewise also the chief priests mocking him with the scribes and elders, said . . . he trusted in God: let him deliver him" (Matt. 27:39-44). Also Matt. 26: 67, 68; Mark 15:14, 19.

F. *Smitten:*
"They shall *smite* the Judge of Israel with a rod, upon the cheek" (Micah 5:1). Also Isa. 50:6; 53:4; Zech. 13:6, 7; Lam. 3:30.

F. "And took the reed and smote him on the head" (Matt. 27:30). Also Matt. 26:67, 68; Luke 22:63; Mark 14:27; 15:19; John 1:3.

G. *Spit Upon:*
". . . I hid not my face from shame and spitting" (Isa. 50:6).

G. "And some began to spit on him, and to cover his face, and to buffet him" (Mark 14:65).

H. *Crucified:*
"They pierced my hands and my feet" (Ps. 22:16).

H. "They crucified him" (John 19:18). Also John 20:25.

I. *Like Transgressors:*
"He was numbered with the transgressors" (Isa. 53:12).

I. "And with him they crucify two thieves. And the scripture was fulfilled which saith, And he was numbered with the transgressors" (Mark 15:27, 28).

J. *Suffered for our sins:*
"Surely he hath borne *our* griefs, and carried *our* sorrows . . . he was wounded for *our* transgressions, he was bruised for *our* iniquities . . . the Lord hath laid on him the iniquity of *us* all" (Isa. 53:4-6). Also Isa. 53:8, 12; Dan. 9:26.

J. "The next day John seeth Jesus coming unto him, and saith, Behold the Lamb of God, which taketh away the sin of the world" (John 1:29). Also Matt. 20:28; Heb. 9:28; 10:10; I Peter 3:18.

K. *Resurrection:*
"Neither wilt thou suffer thine Holy One to see corruption" (Ps. 16:10). Also Ps. 49:15; 71:20; Isa. 25:8.

K. "He is not here, but is risen . . . And their eyes were opened, and they saw him; and he vanished out of their sight . . . The Lord is risen indeed" (Luke 24:6, 31, 34). Also Acts 2:31; I Cor. 15:5-9; (and in Matt., Mark, and John).

I have quoted but a few of the numerous predictions and fulfilments in regard to the Messiah. Anyone who would wish to have more identification marks as to the Messiahship of Jesus will find them throughout the New Testament and compare them with the Old Testament. This wonder of Prophecy and its fulfilment, centuries later, has amazed all Bible students. I shall quote here the words of one of these students who, in a way, expresses the feelings of all who stood baffled at this miracle:

"Centuries before Christ was born His birth and career, His sufferings and glory, were all described in outline and detail in the Old Testament. Christ is the only Person ever born into this world whose ancestry, birth-time, forerunner, birth-place, birth-manner, infancy, manhood, teaching, character, career, preaching, reception, rejection, death, burial, resurrection and ascension were all prewritten in the most marvelous manner centuries before He was born.

"Who could draw a picture of a man not yet born? Surely God, and God alone. Nobody knew 500 years ago that Shakespeare was going to be born; or 250 years ago that Napoleon was to be born. Yet here in the Bible we have the most striking and unmistakable likeness of a Man portrayed, not by one, but by twenty or twenty-five artists, none of whom had ever seen the Man they were painting." *Canon Dyson Hague*

In short, Jesus, and He alone, has produced the perfect credentials and thus established His identity as Messiah-Saviour. No one before Him nor after Him has done that; nor could there be anyone in the future able to do it.

Chapter XVIII

CHRISTIANITY IS COMPLETED JUDAISM

We have seen that the two main objections of the Jews[1] against Christianity have been (1) that Jesus was not the Messiah of whom the Torah (Old Testament) spoke and whom the Jews expected to fulfill the ancient prophecies and (2) that the dogmas of Christianity are contrary to those of Judaism. They maintain that the doctrines of the Trinity and the divinity of the Messiah are pure idolatry, and in contradiction to the Jewish belief in One God. To these objections, as well as to others, such as the "Virgin Birth," "Original Sin," "Vicarious Atonement," there is but one answer: Christianity not only does not oppose basic Judaism but it is Judaism itself fulfilled.

We can show the Jew that Jesus of Nazareth was the true Messiah because in Him all prophecies regarding the Messiah were fulfilled, although some individuals or groups of Jews may have expected something else. We can show him that those doctrines which are now known as "Christian Doctrines" are typically Jewish. Like Philip (John 1:45) we can tell the Jew: "We have found Him of whom Moses in the law and the prophets did write." *Jesus, the Messiah (Jeshuah Hamashiach) in the Old Testament:*

The portrait of Jesus as the promised Saviour is clearly outlined in the Torah from its first book to its last. Already in Eden after the fall of Adam God promised that the seed of the woman would ultimately crush the head of the Serpent, Satan (Genesis 3:15), and thus bring about the redemption of fallen humanity. Till that time Satan had many a chance to "bruise mankind." Thus already during the time of Noah the human race had become so degraded and corrupt that God had to destroy it by the flood. He saved only God-fearing Noah and his family. Humanity fell

---

[1] We mean those Jews who speak as Jews. The contentions and objections of liberal Jews and the like, are not Jewish (from a Jewish viewpoint) but are common to liberal Gentiles and should be dealt with as with Gentiles.

more and more away from its creator, yet He would no longer
destroy His handiwork so He called Abraham out of his corrupt
surroundings to train him and his descendants to be a people who
would be a blessing to all mankind (Genesis 12:1-3).

This was the birth of the "Covenant" between God and the
Jewish people, the covenant which the Jews, as frail human beings,
have often violated but which God the Almighty, all merciful, un-
changeable has repeatedly ratified. This seed of Abraham that
was to become a blessing and salvation to the world, was begun in
Isaac; as Jesus later, he, too, had a miraculous birth, since Sarah
could not naturally bear a child (Genesis 17:15-19; and Genesis
21:12). Isaac so loved God that he was ready to be sacrificed to
Him. The Covenant was later confirmed with Jacob and his seed
— not with Esau (Genesis 28:13, 14). Of Jacob's descendants, the
twelve tribes, the tribe of Judah was distinguished as the kingly
line through whom the Messiah would come (Genesis 49:8, 10).
Of this royal family came David and later, at the appointed time,
Jesus, the "Son of David." In the previous chapter we have given
a list of prophecies which tell the life story of Jesus in the Old
Testament.

Many of the rabbis, in their antagonism to Christianity or in
their zeal to preserve their particular kind of Judaism, have applied these passages to others rather than to the Messiah. But
it is easy to show how wrong they were. Indeed, many Jewish
authorities of highest standing clearly and boldly taught that they
refer to the Messiah, and these have been generally recognized
by the Jews.

Jewish Exegetes Conform with Christian Interpretation:

Let us cite here a few of these controversial passages:

The "Seed of the Woman" that shall bruise the serpent's head
(Genesis 3:15) is, according to Christian belief, the Messiah who
would destroy the power of Satan. Many Rabbis deny that, but
the ancient, most authoritative Jewish exegetes and expositors of
the Bible such as the Targums, the Midrashim and others, plainly
taught that this "seed" is the Messiah.

"And I will put enmity between thee and the *woman*, and between the seed of thy sons, and between the *seed* of her sons: and
it shall be when the sons of the *woman* keep the commandments
of the *law*, they will be prepared to smite thee on thy *head*; but
if they forsake the commandments of the *law*, thou wilt be prepared to wound them in the heel. Nevertheless for them there

shall be a *medicine:* and they shall make a *remedy* for the heel in the days of the *King Messiah*" (Targum Jerusalem).

"As thou wentest forth for the *salvation of the people* by the hands of the *Mashiach,* the *Son of David,* who shall *wound Satan* who is the head, the King and Prince of the house of the wicked, and shall *raze up* (overturn) all his strength, power, policy and dominion" (R. David Kimchi).

"As the incarnation of evil *Satan* is the arch-enemy of the *Messiah: he* is anti-Christ. The light which was created before the world, was hidden by God beneath *his* throne; and to the question of *Satan* in regard to it God answered: 'This light is kept for *Him* who shall bring thee to shame.' At his request God showed *Satan* the Messiah; and when he saw *Him,* he trembled, fell upon his face, and cried: 'Verily this is the Messiah, who shall hurl (bruise) me, and all the princes of the *angels* of the peoples down even into hell" (Pesikta Rab. 3:6, ed. Friedmann, p. 161, b).

"This is that *seed* that is coming from another place, And who is this? This is the *King* Messiah" (Ber. Rabbah, 51, ed. Wars, p. 95, a, on Genesis 19:23).

When Eve bore her first son she called him Cain and said, "I have gotten a man from the Lord" (that is what the name means). This verse may be translated variously: "I have obtained a man-God." According to the ancient Rabbis (in Midrash) Eve thought this son was the "seed," the Messiah who would defeat Satan.

The "seed" of Abraham (Genesis 22:18) is also applied to the Messiah by the ancient Rabbis. This was also their interpretation of the "seed" of Jacob in Genesis 28:14 (John 8:56-58; and Hebrews 2:16).

Of the "star out of Jacob" (Numbers 24:17) the Jerusalem Targum says: "When the mighty King of Jacob's house shall reign and the Messiah the Power-Sceptre of Israel be anointed He shall slay the Princes of Moab. From them their King shall arise and their Redeemer be of them." The Princes of Moab here are symbols of the power of Satan. Remember what havoc they have wrought in Israel (see Numbers 25:1-19). Other books which are most sacred to the Jewish people also declare that this "Star of Jacob" refers to the Messiah. So Targum, Onkelos, Pesikta, the Sohar, Debarim, Rabbah and others, The Pesikta, for instance, says: "Our Rabbis have a tradition that in the week in which the

Messiah will be born there will be a bright Star in the east, which is the 'Star of the Messiah.' "[2]

Shiloh:

A very important passage is Genesis 49:10: "The sceptre shall not depart from Judah nor a Law-giver from between his feet until *Shiloh* come." Christians understand that Shiloh here refers to Messiah, and they justly argue, if Jesus was not the Messiah, who was? He must have come before the Sceptre departed from Judah. To refute this argument some modern Rabbis assert that Shiloh does not refer to Messiah but to a certain place called Shiloh.

However, the ancient Jewish expositors and commentaries understand it as referring to Messiah. For instance, Jerusalem Targum, says: "Kings shall not cease from the house of Judah . . . until the time that the King Messiah shall come. . . ."

Divinity of Messiah:

Some Rabbis say that the idea of the Messiah as a divine being is foreign to Judaism. The Rambam taught that there is nothing supernatural in the person of the Messiah or in his deeds. They find it difficult to explain Jeremiah 23:5, 6: "Behold, the days come, saith the Lord, that I will raise unto David a righteous Branch, and a King shall reign and prosper, and shall execute judgment and justice in the earth. In his days Judah shall be saved and Israel shall dwell safely: and this is his name whereby he shall be called, THE LORD OUR RIGHTEOUSNESS," where the Bible says that He the Branch of David shall be called *Jehovah — Our Righteousness.* Here again the ancient Jewish sages taught that it refers to Messiah.

In the Midrash on Lamentations 1:16 we read: "What is the name of the King Messiah? Rabbi Abba, son of Kahana said, 'Jehovah' for it is written: This is His name, whereby He shall be called, 'Jehovah our Righteousness.' " The Messiah's divine attributes are also portrayed in Micah 5:2 — "whose origin is of old from eternity." The Jerusalem Targum explains: "Out of thee Bethlehem shall Messiah go forth before me to exercise dominion over Israel; whose name has been spoken from of old from the day of eternity."

So also Malachi 3:1 refers to Messiah. Eben Ezra explains here: "The Lord is both the Divine Majesty and the Angel of the Covenant." Kimchi says: "The Lord is the King Messiah; He is also the Angel of the Covenant."

[2] In this connection you may quote Matthew 2:2, 9 and Revelation 22:16.

Isaiah 9:6 plainly foretells the coming of the Redeemer the "Mighty God" — etc. Yet the later controversial rabbis insist that a Messiah-God (divine) is not in conformity with the Jewish Torah. But the Jerusalem Targum and the Midrash (on Deuteronomy 2:4) refer this verse to Messiah. *Son of God* — "I will declare the decree: the LORD hath said unto me, Thou art my Son; this day have I begotten thee" (Psalm 2:7).

When John the Baptist spoke to the Jewish crowds around saying, "and I saw and bear record that this is the Son of God" (John 1:34): Or when Paul preached Christ in the synagogues, declaring that "He is the *Son of God*" (Acts 9:10; 13:33; Hebrews 5:5), the Jews did not find anything foreign in the term "son of God." Only later to counteract Christian influence did some Rabbis say that Psalm 2 does not apply to Messiah and that the Hebrew words "nashku bar" do not mean "kiss the son" but something else. .But the ancient Jewish exegetes (the Targums, the Talmud, etc.) understood that this chapter refers to Messiah. The "Holy Zohar" says: "This is the faithful shepherd; of thee it is said, 'Kiss the Son'; thou art the Prince of the Israelites, the Lord of the earth . . . the Son of the Most High, the Son of the Holy God . . . and gracious Shekinah."

Another stumbling-block which the later rabbis placed in the way of evangelization of the Jews is the Virgin Birth.

The Virgin Birth:

"Therefore the Lord himself shall give you a sign; Behold, a virgin shall conceive and bear a son, and shall call his name Immanuel" (Isaiah 7:14). This passage proves that the Messiah was to be born of a virgin. The later rabbis say that the word *almah* of that verse does not mean virgin but young woman and that the whole passage does not refer to the Messiah but to some contemporary event.

That the Hebrew word *almah* means virgin has always been understood until the controversial rabbis tried to change its meaning, and so also was it understood by the ancient authorities that this verse refers to Messiah.

Messiah a King:

"Rejoice greatly, O daughter of Zion; shout, O daughter of Jerusalem: behold thy King cometh unto thee: he is just and having salvation; lowly, and riding upon an ass, and upon a colt the foal of an ass" (Zechariah 9:9).

Midrash Koheleth (63:2) says: "As it is of the former Redeemer — And Moses took his wife and his sons and set them on an ass (Exodus 4:20) so it is said of the latter Redeemer (Messiah), 'Poor and riding on an ass.'"

Rabbi Saadiah Gaon (on Daniel) says, "But is it not written of the Messiah, 'Lowly and riding upon an ass'? Yes, but this shows that He will come in humility and not in pride upon horses."

A Prophet Like Moses:

"The Lord thy God will raise up unto thee a Prophet from the midst of thee, of thy brethren, like unto me; unto him ye shall hearken" (Deuteronomy 18:15). Commenting on this verse, Rabbi Levi Ben Gershon says: "In fact the Messiah is such a Prophet as it is stated in the Midrash on the verse, 'Behold my servant shall prosper' — Moses by the miracles which he wrought drew but a single nation to the worship of God, but the Messiah will draw all nations to the worship of God."

Melchizedek (a Priest):

"The LORD hath sworn, and will not repent. Thou art a priest forever after the order of Melchizedek" (Psalm 110:4). The whole chapter is applied to Messiah by the Targums and Midrash and later commentators.

Despised and Rejected:

Isaiah 53. One of the objections the rabbis have against Jesus is that the expected Messiah was to be a mighty king who would overthrow the Gentile rule, and instead would let Israel rule over all nations. Jesus, they say, did not satisfy those longings and expectations. On the contrary He was despised and rejected and executed like a mean criminal.

When the Evangelists, Matthew (21:42), Mark (8:31) and Luke (17:24, 25) reminded the Jewish people that He was destined to be rejected, to suffer and to be killed, it was not strange to Jewish ears. They knew what Isaiah in chapter 53 meant; they knew that it applies to Messiah. So did also the later commentators as the Jerusalem Targum and the "Holy Zohar." Rabbi Saadiah Ibn Danan comments: "There is a secret one (interpretation) sealed up in its midst, which sees throughout allusions to the King Messiah . . . and in the same verse it is expounded by our Rabbis."

Rabbi Moshen Alsheck says: "Our Rabbis with one voice accept and affirm the opinion that the prophet is here speaking of the Messiah." Today the rabbis speak differently.

In view of the "Suffering Messiah" as portrayed in Isaiah 53, etc., some rabbis propounded the theory that there were to be two Messiahs: one Messiah being Ben Joseph of the Joseph dynasty. He is to suffer and die; the other Messiah Ben David, of the Davidic dynasty. He is to come as mighty King and ruler of the whole world. Thus R. Kimchi quotes R. Abraham Eben Ezra who writes that this prophecy "applies to the great wars which shall be in all the world in the days of the Messiah the Son of Joseph." The Messiah therefore is the person to be smitten "before the scattering of the sheep." On verse 53:12 the Jerusalem Targum says: "He, Messiah, shall intercede for man's sins, and the rebellions for His sake shall be forgiven."

So also the Midrash B'reshith Rabbah: "And when Israel is sinful, the Messiah seeks for mercy upon them, as it is written, 'By His stripes' we were healed, and He carried the sins of many, and made intercession for the transgressors."

Those rabbis who do not like the traditional interpretation of Isaiah 53 which affirms that it applies to Messiah, say that it may apply to someone else (contemporary) or to Israel as the suffering servant of God. Of course, any Jew who knows Hebrew (or in translation) will on reading this chapter at once see that it cannot apply to the Jewish people, nor to any individual before Jesus. 1. The Jews were not punished for the sins of others. The Jews in their prescribed prayers confess their sins and those of their fathers, for which they have been punished. 2. No Jew would say that his people is without sin, while the person in Isaiah 53 is sinless. 3. This person submits to His suffering and death without protest or resistance. This cannot be said of the Jews. 4. He was killed and buried. This cannot be said of the Jewish people as a whole. That Isaiah did not think that the Jews were a sinless people one may see in his first chapter — "Ah sinful nation, a people laden with iniquity, etc."

Pierced:

John (the evangelist, in 19:34-37) when relating how Jesus was pierced quotes Zechariah 12:10, "And I will pour upon the house of David, and upon the inhabitants of Jerusalem, the spirit of grace and of supplications: and they shall look upon me whom they have pierced, and they shall mourn for him, as one mourneth for his only son, and shall be in bitterness for him, as one that is in bitterness for his firstborn," as a prophecy which was then fulfilled. While modern rabbis do not admit that this passage applies to Messiah, the old commentators said that it does apply to Messiah. So, for example, R. Kimchi, Abarbanel, and Yarchi.

Rabbi Alshech says: "They shall lift up their eyes to me in perfect repentance, when they see Him whom they have pierced, that is Messiah, son of Joseph." By "they" the rabbis mean the Gentile nations who would kill this Messiah Ben Joseph in the war of Gog and Magog, but they agree that it refers to a Messiah who would be killed. ("The Lord said unto my Lord, Sit thou at my right hand, until I make thine enemies thy footstool" — Psalm 110:1). This verse is cited by Jesus as referring to Him (Matthew 22: 41-45). Modern rabbis would not admit that it refers to the Messiah. The ancients did so, however. Thus Midrash Tehillim on Psalm 2 says, "The affairs of the Messiah are told in the Torah (Pentateuch) — Exodus 4:22, in the Prophets — Isaiah 53:13, and in the Hagiographa — Psalm 110:1." So also Midrash on Psalm 18:35, "Thou hast also given me the shield of thy salvation; and thy right hand hath holden me up, and thy gentleness hath made me great."

Rabbi Yoden in the name of Rabbi Kama said that in the future to come in the days of the Messiah, the Holy One blessed be He, will make the Messiah to sit at His right hand as it is said, "The Lord said unto my Lord, Sit thou at my right hand." And so also Rabbi Saadia Gaon (on Daniel 7:13): "And this is the Messiah our Righteousness, as it is said, 'The Lord said unto my Lord, Sit on my right hand until I make thine enemies thy footstool.'"

Coming Again:

"I saw in the night visions, and, behold, one like the Son of man came with the clouds of heaven, and came to the Ancient of days, and they brought him near before him. And there was given him dominion, and glory, and a kingdom, that all people, nations, and languages should serve him: his dominion is an everlasting dominion which shall not pass away, and his kingdom that which shall not be destroyed" (Daniel 7:13, 14). Jesus, and later the apostles, cited this passage as applying to Him (Matthew 26: 64; Mark 13:36; Revelation 1:7; 14:14).

This passage, too, contrary to objecting rabbis, the ancient commentators applied to the Messiah. The Talmud, Sanhedrin 98:1 says, "R. Alexander said R. Joshua Ben Levi objects to what is written. 'And behold one like the Son of Man came with the clouds of Heaven'; and it is written, 'Poor and riding on an ass'; if they (Israel) are worthy He (messiah) comes with the clouds of Heaven; but if they are not worthy, He comes poor and riding on an ass."

Abarbanel: The expositor explains these words "Like the Son of Man" as referring to King Messiah.

Rabbi Shimeon bar Yochai: "When the King Messiah shall be revealed all the nations of the world shall be gathered to Him."

I have thus cited but a few of the many comments of the most authoritative rabbis who have interpreted the Scriptures in the same manner as have the Christians, and not as do the modern rabbis. The few examples I cited here are enough to convince the skeptical Jew that true Christianity is not foreign to true Judaism, but they are one and the same religion based on the "Old Testament" Scriptures.

CHAPTER XIX

HEBREW VOCABULARY

INTRODUCTION

This Vocabulary is designed for those who would and should be acquainted with the words and phrases (mostly of religious or ritual nature) which are common among the Jewish people. Since most of these expressions are in Hebrew, I feel it necessary to have here some remarks as to the pronunciation and transliteration of the Hebrew.

A. PRONUNCIATION. There are two main pronunciations: 1. The *Sephardi* Pronunciation, which has been in use among Oriental Jews, and 2. The *Ashkenazi* Pronunciation, used by Occidental (European and American) Jews. Since the *Sephardi* Pronunciation has been introduced in Israel, the Jews in diaspora, too, are gradually adopting this pronunciation. Thus, in this vocabulary, we also follow their example, but we give in brackets also the *Ashkenazi* Pronunciation form if it is still widely in use.

The main differences in the two pronunciations are:

1. The unstressed consonant *tav* is pronounced by the *Ashkenazi* like "s," while the *Sephardi* pronounce it like "th." (Thus, in *Sephardi: ba"ith;* in *Ashkenazi: ba"is).*

2. The long vowel *kammatz*, which in *Sephardi* is "ah," is in *Ashkenazi*, "uh" (or "oh"). (Thus, in *Sephardi, aron;* but in *Ashkenazi, uh"rn*).

3. The accent. According to the *Sephardi* pronunciation, the accent generally comes on the last syllable of the word, except when the last vowel sounds are "ee" or "ai." In the *Ashkenazi* pronunciation, the accent generally comes on the next to the last syllable.

(We shall indicate the accent in the *Ashkenazi* pronunciation, which comes in brackets, as well as the exceptions in the *Sephardi* pronunciation by ["].)

172

(As a whole the *Ashkenazi* pronounces the words somewhat negligently. Only the stressed vowel is well recognized; the others are not quite distinguishable. So *"chanukkah"* becomes to *Ashkenazi, cha"n-k-; milchamah" — mlchu"m-).*

B. TRANSLITERATION. Many of the Hebrew letters have no equivalent or counterpart in the English alphabet. Yet, disregarding the complicated rules, signs and symbols of grammarians, we have tried here to simplify the transliteration of Hebrew into English so that the reader may be enabled to pronounce the words at least approximately like the Jews do it (and incidentally, the Jews vary in pronunciation of the Hebrew in accordance with their various vernaculars).

The following few rules may be of help in reading the words of our vocabulary correctly:

1. Hebrew has *no silent letters;* every vowel as well as consonant is distinctly pronounced.
2. *G* is always *G,* as in give, get, good.
3. *Th* is pronounced as in thin, both.
4. *Y* is always a consonant, as in Yes, You.
5. *Tz* is like the German *Z* (in Zwei, ZU"RICH).
6. *Ch* is a guttural sound equivalent to the German in *ach, bach,* and the *Scottish* in *loch.*
7. The vowels:

a=as in arm, far	Diphthongs:
e=as in get, end	a'a like two a-a
i=as in in, pity	ai like ah+i
o=as in lord, orbit	ei like eh+i
u=as in put, or as *oo* in noon.	
uh long u as in food.	

8. (") Indicates where the accent should be.
9. (') Indicates that some vowel is omitted; it serves also as a secondary accent.
10. Affixes to a word are shown in non-capital letters: for example haKOHEN — the Kohen; l'SHANAH — to a year; uBRACHAH — and a blessing; v'ATTAH — and you (u, or v prefixing a word means "and").

There is no indefinite article in Hebrew.

The Hebrew letter *kaf* is generally pronounced like *k,* sometimes it is pronounced like the guttural *cheth,* and in that case we represent it by *ch* (as in *loch*).

HEBREW VOCABULARY

Mostly of Religious Significance Often Used By Jews in Common Parlance

ADON, Master, Lord. Thus *Adon Olam,* Lord of the Universe (God). In modern Hebrew also, Mister.

ADONAI, God. Notice, the word is a plural noun, and literally means: "My lords."

AGGADAH (aguh"de), Narrative, legend, allegory. The non-legal portions of the Talmudic literature.

AGMATH NE"FESH (ag"mes-ne"fesh), Grief, deep sorrow.

AGUNAH, A woman, whose husband deserted her, or whose husband's death cannot be legally established.

AIN HARAA (anne ho"rre), "Evil-Eye."

ALAV HASHALOM (uh"lev hashuh"lem), "Peace be upon him"; expression used after mentioning the name of a departed person.

ALEF BEITH (aleph bais), Alphabet.

ALMAN, Widower.

ALMANAH, Widow.

AM haARETZ (amme uh"retz), Literally: "people of the land." An ignoramus, a crude person.

APIKO"RES, Atheist; skeptic.

ARBA KANFOTH, Literally: "four corners." See *Tallith Kattan.*

ARON (uh"rn), Chest, ark; coffin.

ARON haKo"DESH (uh"rn koi'desh), The "Holy Ark" where the sacred scrolls are kept (at the synagogue).

ASHKENAZIM, Term applied to the descendants of the so-called "German Jews." These include all European Jews (and those that emigrated from Europe), excepting those of Spanish Jewish origin, who are called *Sephardim.*

ASSARAH b'TEVETH (asuh"re btai'ves), See chapter on "Feasts and Fasts."

ASSE"RETH haDIBROTH (assei"rs hadib"res), The Ten Commandments.

ASSE"RETH Y'MAI T'SHUVAH (assei"rs y'mai tshi"ve), "Ten Days of Penitence." See chapter on "Feasts and Fasts."

AVEIL (uh"vl), Mourner. See *Shiv'ah.*

AVEIRAH, Transgression, sin.

AVODAH ZARAH (avoi"de zuh"re), Foreign (strange) worship, i.e., idol worship, idolatry.

BA'AL BA"YITH (balebus"), Owner of a house, or boss.

BA'AL BRITH (ba'al bris), Father of the boy at the circumcision ceremony; also ally; and confederate.

BA'AL CHAI, Living creature.

BA'AL CHOV, Debtor.

BA'AL KORE, Lector, reader of the scroll of the Torah at the service in the synagogue.

BA'AL MAZZAL (or BAR MAZZAL), A fortunate man.

BA'AL M'LACHAH, Artisan.

BA'AL MUM, Cripple.

BA'AL NESS, One used to miracles; miracle worker.

BA'AL SHEM, Miracle worker (by the power of the Divine Name).

BA'AL SIMCHAH, Host of the feast (as at weddings, circumcisions, Bar Mitzvah, and other such joyous occasions).

BA'AL TORAH, Scholar of the Torah.

BA'AL T'FILLAH, Cantor, one who leads in prayer at the synagogue.

BA'AL Tz'DAKAH, Philanthropist.

BADCHAN, Entertainer at weddings.

BETH DIN (bezn), House of law, court house, often: the Rabbinate.

BETH haMIKDASH, The sanctuary, the Holy Temple.

BETH K'VAROTH, Graveyard, cemetery.

BETH KNESSETH (beis aknei"ses), Synagogue.

BETH MIDRASH, Synagogue, where religious books are studied.

BAR MITZVAH, Literally: "Son of Commandment." At the age of 13 the Jewish boy reaches his religious majority. See chapter on "Customs."

BARUCH DAYAM EMMETH (buh"rech da"yen e"mmes), "Blessed be the true Judge"; this formula is to be uttered upon hearing of the death of a Jew.

BARUCH haBA (buhrechab"be), Welcome. (Blessed is he who has just come.)

BARUCH haSHEM, "Thank God." Literally: "Blessed be the Name."

BASAR v'DAM (buh"ser veda"m), "Flesh and blood," mortal man.

BATH MITZVAH, "Daughter of Commandment." See *Bar Mitzah*.

BATLAN, Idler, unpractical person.

b'CHINAM, Free of charge, gratuitously, for nothing, in vain, without cause.

B'CHOR, "First Born," eldest son. (See Exod. 13:2, 12, 13, and Num. 18: 14-16.)

BEMA (or, BIMA, or BAMA), Elevated stage in the synagogue, whereon the scroll of the *Torah* is placed when it is being read.

B'NAI BRITH, pl., Sons of the Covenant; name of well-known Jewish fraternity.

BEN YACHID (yuh"ched), "The only son."

b'EZRATH haSHEM (see *haShem*), "With God's Help."

B'HEIMAH, Cattle, beast; used to describe a dull-witted person.

B'LI NEI"DER, "Without Vow."

BRACHAH (bruh"che), Blessing, benediction.

BRITH (briss), Short for *Brith Milah* — Covenant of Circumcision. Denotes ceremony of circumcision.

BRITH CHADASHA, "New Covenant" — The New Testament.

CHACHAM (chuh"chem), Sage, wise man. Title of Sephardie Rabbi.

CHAGA (cho"gge), A non-Jewish festival (used disparagingly).

CHALLAH, (1) Loaf of white bread, usually in braided form. (2) The priest's share of the dough. See Numbers 15:20-21.

CHAMETZ (chum"ets), Leaven. Term applied to all leavened food and objects that come in close contact with leaven.

CHATHAN (chuh"sn), Bridegroom.

CHATHUNAH (chas"sene), Wedding.

CHAVEIR (chav"r), Friend, associate, companion, mate, member.

CHAZIR (chazr), Swine, pig; pork. (The most objectionable food to the Jew.)

CHAZZAN (chazn), Cantor.

CHEI"DER, "Room"; religious elementary school.

CHEI'REM, Ban, excommunication.

CHESHBON, Reckoning, account, calculation, bill, arithmetic.

CHESHBON haNEFESH, Moral stocktaking, introspection.

CHEVRAH (see *Chaveir*), Company, society, association.

CHILLUL haSHEM (see *haShem*), Desecration of the Divine Name. (See *Kiddush haShem*.)

CHOCHMAH, Wisdom, prudence, popularly: a wise saying, a bright idea.

CHO"DESH, "New," term applied to the New Moon, month.

CHUMASH, The Pentateuch, The Five Books of Moses.

CHURBAN (chor"bn), Ruin, destruction; often used as short of *Churban Beth haMikdash*, "The Destruction of The Temple."

CHUPPAH, Wedding canopy.

CHUTZPAH, Impudence, boldness.

DAYAN, Rabbinic Judge.

DIN, Law, judgment. The commandments as interpreted by the Rabbis.

DIBBUK, Ghost possessing man's body.

EIDUTH (ei"ds), Testimony; witness.

EI"SHETH ISH (aishes ish), Married woman, another man's wife.

EITZAH, Advice, counsel.

EMETH, (em"es), Truth.

EMUNAH, Faith.

ELOHIM, God. The Hebrew word *Elohim* is a plural noun, which means "Gods" and suggests the plurality of the Godhead. So also *Adonai*, which refers to God, is in the plural and means "my Lords."

ELOKIM, In order not to take the name of the Lord in vain, the Jew, when not in prayer, would use *Elokim* instead of the sacred name *Elohim*.

ERETZ ISRAEL, Land of Israel.

EREV SHABBATH, The day preceding the Shabbath.

EREV PE"SSACH, The day before *Pessach*.

GABBAI (gab"be), Collector, treasurer.

GALUTH (guh"les), Exile.

GAM ZU l'TOVAH, "This, too, is for the good."

GANAV (gan"ef), Thief, cheat, crook.

GAN E"DEN (g'nai"dem), Paradise.

GAON, (guh"en), Genius. Renowned and learned Rabbi.

GAZLAN, Robber, brigand.

GEHE"NNOM, Hell.

GER, Proselyte. A Gentile converted to Judaism.

GET, Divorce.

GEULAH, Redemption (usually refers to the coming of the Messiah).

G'MARA, The usual name for the Talmud.

GO″LEM (goi″lm), Shapeless matter. Clumsy, awkward person. (Legendary human formed of clay, Robot.)

GORAL (goi″rl), Lot, portion, fortune, fate.

GOY, Non-Jew, Gentile. Popularly also: an ignorant or unobservant Jew.

HACHNASATH ORCHIM (hachnuh″ses orchim), "Bringing in the guests"; hospitality.

HAGGADAH (haguh″de), "Narrative" (see also Aggadah). The story of the Deliverance from Egypt, as recited, from the book by that name, on the Eve of Passover.

haKADOSH BARUCH HU (hakuh″desh bor″che), "The Holy One, Blessed Be His Name." One of the names the Jew uses for "God."

HAL′VAY, Interjection: Oh that, would that, "I wish that it be so."

haSHEM, "The Name." God's proper name, the Tetragrammaton, which is written in Hebrew by the four letters Yod Hei Vav Hei, and pronounced in English "Jehovah," is never uttered by the Jew. When he meets with that name while reading the Bible, or at prayer he substitutes (pronounces it) the word Adonai, otherwise he uses instead the word haShem — "The Name" — often with the addition of Yith-barech — "Blessed be He." Thus b'Ezrath haShem, Baruch haShem, L′ma″an haShem — "for the sake of God."

haTIKVAH, "The Hope." Generally applied to the Hebrew national anthem.

HATZLACHAH (hatzluh″che), Success, luck, prosperity, good fortune.

HAVDALAH (see l'Havdil) (havduh″le), "Separation." Benediction over a cup of wine at the conclusion of the Sabbath and Festivals, thus separating the sanctity of the holy day from the routine of the week days. See chapter on "Feasts and Fasts."

HAZKARATH N'SHAMOTH (hazko″res nesho″mes), "The remembering of the souls." The prayer for the departed souls (also called Yizkor), which is solemnly recited in the synagogue on Yom Kippur and on the three Pilgrim Festivals. See chapter on "Customs."

HECHSHER, A permit issued by a rabbi certifying that a certain food product is ritually fit to be eaten.

HEFKER, Ownerless property, lawlessness, anarchy.

HESPED, Funeral oration, obituary.

HETTER, "Loosening," legal permission.

HETTER HORA′AH″, Authorization to function as rabbi.

IM YIRTZE haSHEM (mer″tsheshem), "If God wills." See haShem.

IVRI, Hebrew, Jew.

IVRITH, The Hebrew language.

KA″AS, Anger, vexation (grief).

KABBALAH (kabuh″leh), Receipt, tradition. See chapter on "Kabbalah."

KABBALATH PANIM (kabuh″les puh″nem), Welcoming, reception.

KABTZAN, Pauper, a poor man. In Yiddish, also: "A Shnorrer."

KADDISH, Prayer recited by mourners during the first eleven months after death of a near relative.

KADOSH (kuh″dish), Holy, sacred, saint.

KALLAH (kal″e), Bride.

KAMTZAN, Miser.

KAPPARAH (Kapuh″re), Atonement, expiation, expiatory-sacrifice. An animal used as a vicarious sacrifice on the day before Yom Kippur (Day of Atonement). See chapter on "Feasts and Fasts."

KAROV (kuh″ref), Near relative.

KASHER (kuh″shr), Fit, proper. See chapter on "Customs" (section Kosher).

KASHYA (kash″e), "Difficulty," popularly: a difficult question.

KAVANAH (kavuh″ne), Devotion, intention, attention, meaning.

KAVOD (kuv″ed), Honor, dignity, glory, majesty, respect.

KEI′VER, Grave, sepulchre.

KELEV, Dog, disparagingly used for wicked person.

K'HILLAH (also KAHAL) (kuhl), Congregation, community, assembly.

KIBBUTZ, Gathering, company; in Israel: a group of settlers organized on a cooperative basis.

KIDDUSH, "Sanctification." Benediction for the sanctification of Sabbaths and Festivals over a cup of wine.

KIDDUSH haSHEM, "Sanctification of the Name" (God's Name). A good deed performed by a Jew that arouses praise and commendation by Gentiles is considered as a tribute to God. God is glorified by the acts of His people. To die for *Kiddush haShem* has been considered as the supreme merit (sacrifice) See *Chillul haShem*.

KISHUF, Witchcraft, sorcery, magic.

K'LALAH (kluh"le), Curse.

KOHEN, Priest, a descendant of Aaron, brother of Moses.

KORBAN, Sacrifice.

KRIA'A", "Rending," tearing. As a sign of grief the mourner, upon hearing of the death of a near relative (parent, son) makes an incision (rend) in the upper corner of his coat (usually at the lapel), and utters the benediction: "*Baruch Dayan Emeth*" (see Joel 2:13).

K'RIATH SH'MA'A" (krish"me), "The Reading of Sh'ma." ("Sh'ma Israel.") *Sh'ma'a"* ("hear") is the first word of the verse: "Hear O Israel: The Lord our God, the Lord is One" (Deut. 6:14). This is considered as the Jewish confession of faith.

K'THUBAH (ksi"be), Marriage contract.

LAMDAN, Learned man, scholar (especially in rabbinic lore).

LA"MED VAV TZADIKIM, "36 Righteous." (The popular belief is that there are at least 36 righteous Jews in every generation without whose merit the world would perish.)

LASHON HARA' (luh"shn horr"e), "Bad tongue," evil talk, calumny, gossip.

LASHON KO"DESH (luh"shn koi"dish), The "Sacred Tongue," Hebrew.

l'CHAYIM, "To life": The customary salutation (toast) among Jews when imbibing some alcoholic beverage (usually on festive occasions).

LEVI (lai"veh), Levite; of the tribe of Levi. As to the original functions of Kohen and Levi see Numbers 18; Deuteronomy 10:8-9, 18; Nehemiah 10:35-40.

l'HAVDIL, To differentiate. See *Havdalah*.

L'MA"AN haSHEM, "For the sake of God." See *haShem*.

l'SHANAH TOVAH (l'shuh"ne toi"ve), "To a good year." (Equivalent to:

"Happy New Year.") See chapter on "Feasts and Fasts."

LU"ACH, Board, tablet, schedule, calendar.

L'VAYAH, Funeral.

MA'ARIV, The Evening Prayer. One of the three daily prayers.

MA'ASEH, Story, tale. Deed.

MACHSHEIFAH, Witch, sorceress.

MACHZOR, Prayer book for holidays.

MAGEIFAH, Plague, epidemic.

MAGEN DAVID, "Shield of David" Sexagram.

MAKKOTH (singular MAKKAH) or MALKOTH, Beating, blows, plagues.

MAL'ACH, Angel, messenger.

MAL'ACH haMA"VETH, The Angel of Death.

MAMZER, Bastard, illegitimate child.

MASHI"ACH, "Anointed" Messiah.

MASHKON, Security pledge.

MASKIL, A wise man, enlightened, cultured.

MATTANAH, Gift, present.

MATZAH, Unleavened bread.

MAZZAL, Luck, fortune.

MAZZAL TOV, "Good luck."

MAZZIK, Injurer; one who causes damage or trouble, demon.

MENORAH, Candlestick, lamp.

METH (mess), Dead; corpse.

M'GILLAH, Roll, scroll; The Book of Esther.

MIKVEH, Reservoir, pool; ritual bath. See chapter on "Synagogue."

MILAH, Circumcision. See chapter on "Customs."

MILCHAMAH, War, fighting, battle.

MINCHAH, (Present gift). The afternoon prayer.

MINHAG, Custom, usage.

MINYA"N, Number, quorum. A quorum of at least ten men over the age of 13 is required to perform public worship.

MISHPACHAH, Family.

MITZVAH, Command, act of charity, pious deed. The rabbis counted 613 Mosaic Commandments (*TaRYaG Mitzvoth*); of these 248 are positive commands ("do's") and 365 negative commands ("don'ts"), i.e. prohibitions.

MIZRACH, East, Orient.

MIZRACHI, A religious-political party in Israel.

MOHEL, Circumciser.

MOSHAV Z'KEINIM, Old people's home.

MOTZAEI SHABBATH, The outgoing of the Sabbath.

M'SHOREIR, Poet.

M'SHUMMAD, Apostate (fem. MESHU-MEDETH), renegade. This word is used as an opprobrious epithet for a Jew who was converted to Christianity.

MUMMAR, Convert, apostate. (See *M'shumad*.)

MUSSAR, Instruction, exhortation.

M'YUCHAS, Of good family, especially of a rabbinic family.

M'ZUZAH, Door post (literally). The word is applied to the parchment scroll which the Jews attach on the right side door post of their dwellings (rooms). The inscriptions on the parchment are: Deut. 6:4-12; 11:13-21.

NACHATH (na"ches), Satisfaction, enjoyment; it refers to pleasure which parents derive from the conduct or happiness of their children.

NADAN, Dowry — trousseau.

NAVI (nu"ve), Prophet.

N'DAVAH (ndu"ve), Alms, donation.

NEIDER, Vow, votive offering.

NIGUN, Melody.

N'SHAMAH, Soul (breath).

N'VEILAH, Carcass, carrion, (a despicable person).

OLAM haBAH, The coming world, eternal life.

OLAM haZEH, This world, carnal life.

PANIM (puh"nem), Face.

PANIM EL PANIM, Face to face.

PARASHAH (par"she), Section, division, subject matter.

PARNASAH, Livelihood, sustenance.

PASUK (puh"sik), A verse of the Bible, sentence.

PASUL (puh"sl), Ritually unfit, disqualified.

PATUR (puh"ter), Acquitter, free.

PEYOTH (pay"es), Sidelock of hair (which is to be left growing).

PEREK, Chapter.

PIKU"ACH NE"FESH, "Saving life." A law may be broken (suspended) if by breaking it, a life may be saved.

PILPUL, Debate, casuistry, sophistical or equivocal reasoning.

P'SHARAH, Compromise, settlement.

RABBI (rebb"e) or RAV (ruf), Master; one learned in Jewish Law.

RACHMANUTH, Mercy, compassion.

R'FUAH, Remedy, cure, medicine.

RASHA (ru"she), Guilty, a wicked person.

RAV (ruf), See *Rabbi*.

RIBONO SHEL OLAM (riboi"ne shel oi"lm), Lord of the Universe.

RU'ACH, Wind, breath, mind, spirit, ghost, disposition.

RUACH haKo"DESH, The Holy Spirit.

ROTZE"IACH, Murderer, (a violent person).

SAR, Chief, leader, nobleman.

SEI"DER, "Order"; the order of home service on Passover Eve.

SEIFER, Book.

SEIFER TORAH, The Book (Scroll) of the Torah.

S'FARADI, See *Ashkenazim*.

SIDDUR, Literally "arrangement," the Jewish prayer book.

SIDRAH (also called PARASHATH ha'-SHAVUAH), The "Weekly Section" (of the Pentateuch read in the synagogue). See CHUMASH.

SIMCHAH, Joy, gladness, festive occasion.

SOFEIR, Writer, scribe, author; copyist of sacred writings on parchment, as the scrolls of the Bible, or the Bible passages of the *Tephilin, Mezuzah*, etc. See chapter on "Synagogue."

SONEI ISRAEL (soi"ne isro"el), Enemy of the Jewish people.

S'UDAH, Meal, dinner, banquet.

SHAB"BES GOI, Epithet for a Gentile who is employed to perform some necessary chores which the Jews are not allowed to do on the Sabbath, such as kindling a light or a fire, or extinguishing it.

SHACHARITH, The morning prayers.

SHACHEN (shuh"chn), Inhabitant, tenant, neighbor.

SHADCHAN, Marriage broker.

SHALI"ACH, Messenger, deputy.

SHALOM, Peace. See *Shalom Alet"-chem*. The common greeting in Israel.

SHALOM ALEI"CHEM, "Peace be unto you" is the usual greeting when Jews meet. The response is: *"Alet"-chem shalom":* "unto you be peace."

SHAMASH, Beadle, attendant, servant. See chapter on "Synagogue."

SHASS, See *Talmud*.

SHED, Demon, devil.

SHE"IVET, Tribe, staff, scepter.

SH'CHINAH, Divine Presence, The *Shechina* Glory. (This word is derived from *Shachan* – to abide, to dwell, to settle down, inhabit.) God as He is revealed to man.

SHIDDUCH, Proposal of marriage. (See *Shadchan*.)

SHIKKOR, Intoxicated, drunkard.

SHIV'AH, Literally, "seven." Denotes seven days of mourning for a near relative. See chapter on "Customs."

SH'MAA ISRAEL, "Hear, O Israel." See *Kriath Sh'ma'a*.

SH'MAD, Apostasy (religious persecution).

S'HMONEH ESREI, Eighteen. The Eighteen Benedictions, together with the *Sh'ma'a Israel* form the most solemn part of the three daily services.

SHOCHET, Slaughterer, one who slaughters animals according to ritual, for Kosher meat consumption. Yiddish: *Shechten*: "to slaughter."

SH'VUAH, Oath.

TA'ANITH (ta"nes), Fast day.

TACHRICHIN, Shrouds.

TALLITH (tal"es), Prayer shawl—a four cornered shawl, to each of which corners *Tzitzith* (fringes) are attached. This shawl is worn over the outer garment during the morning prayer. See Numbers 15:39, 40 and Deuteronomy 22:12. (Besides the *Tallith* which only mature males over the age of 13 wear, there is also the *Tallith Kattan* (the Small *Tallith*, also called *Arba Kanfoth*), which all males, even little boys, have to wear beneath their garments.

TALMID CHACHAM (chu"chem), Wise pupil. (See *Lamdan*.)

TALMUD, Also called G'MARA, or SHASS. (See chapter on "Talmud and Midrash.")

TALMUD TORAH, Jewish religious school.

TANACH, The Bible.

TARGUM, Translation. See *Targum* in chapter on "Exegesis."

TARYAG MITZVOTH, "613 Commands." See *Mitzvah*.

T'CHIATH HAMEITHIM, Resurrection of the dead.

TEIRUTZ (ter"etz), Answer, excuse.

T'FILLAH, Prayer.

T'FILLIN, Phylacteries.

THILIM (til"em), The Psalms of David.

TORAH, Instruction, guidance, learning, law. In its limited sense it means the Five Books of Moses, but usually it connotes the whole Bible (Old Testament) and sometimes it also included all rabbinic writings. See chapter on "Literature."

TREIFAH, Literally: "animal torn by wild beast"; now, forbidden food, not Kosher.

T'SHUVAH, Repentance, answer, return.

TZA'AR, Pain, grief, trouble.

TZADDIK, A righteous, pious person. Often applied to the Chassidic rabbi.

TZARAH, (tzuh"re), Distress, trouble, anguish.

TZ'DAKAH (tzeduh"ke), Charity, alms, righteousness, justice.

TZITZITH, Fringes, tassels. See *Tallith*.

TZ'VA'AH (tzvuh"e), Last will, testament.

VIDDUI, Confession of sins (on the death-bed).

YA"IN NE"SECH, Wine for libation. Wine which was touched by a heathen is forbidden to Jews.

YATHOM (yuh"sm), Orphan (male).

Y'THOMAH (ysoi"me), Female orphan.

YE"ITZER TOV, The good impulse.

YE"ITZER haRA', The evil impulse.

YESHIVAH, (Literally: "sitting"), academy, school of higher Talmudic studies (as the *Che"der* is for elementary Jewish learning).

Y'HUDI, Of the tribe of Judah; now: "Jew."

YICHUS, Pedigree, ancestry, of good family.

YID"DISH, Jewish. This is the language generally used by Eastern European Jews (also long after their settling in other countries). It is a German dialect infused with Hebrew and Slavic elements.

YIZKOR, ("May he remember.") See *Hazkarath N'shamoth*.

Y'MACH SH'MO, "May his name be blotted out," used as a curse.

YOM TOV, A good day – Holiday.

YOVEIL, Jubilee.

Y'RUSHAH, Inheritance.

YORESH, Heir.

Y'SURIM, Affliction, suffering.

Z'CHUTH (z'chuss), Merit.

yarmulka – Skull Cap
– page 98

Z'CHUTH AVOTH (z'chuss o"ves), "The merit of the ancestors," or "for the sake of the forefathers."

Z'MIROTH (z'mee"res), Songs. Traditional hymns sung or chanted during the Sabbath meals.

SUPPLEMENTARY VOCABULARY

The following is a list of Jargonisms used in Jewish speech. Most of them are originated from Hebrew and German.

ALLEVY", It should only be so. I wish it were so.

A-MECHA"YEH, Delicious, wonderful.

AZO'CHUNVAY" (from German *ach und weh*), Woe unto . . .

BER"YEH, Complimentary to an efficient, competent woman.

BOB"BE MA"ASE, Grandmother story; fairy tale, a tall story, hooey.

BALEBO"STEH, Housewife; in a complimentary sense, a fine housekeeper.

F EI'SHIG (see Kosher), Food containing some meat ingredient.

GEFIL"TE FISH, Stuffed fish, a favorite dish, consisting of chopped fish mixed with onions, eggs and seasoning, shaped into balls and cooked in salted water.

GUT, Good; used with salutations as:

GUT SHA"BBES! (May you have a good Sabbath!)

GUT YOM"TOV (May you have a good holiday!)

GUT VOCH (May you have a good week!), a salutation used on Saturday night, when the new week starts.

HALLEVY", See *Allevy*.

HA"MAN-TA"SHEN, A special kind of pastry as a *Purim* treat: (in memory of Haman). They are tri-cornered cakes filled with stewed prunes or poppyseed.

KA"SHA, Porridge, usually of buckwheat. Also used to denote a "mess," a hodge-podge.

KANEHOR"RE, (mixture of German and Hebrew words: *Kein, Ayin-hara'a*): "May no evil eye harm . . . !", often used in Jewish parlance. For example: "He makes a good living. *Kanhorre!*" "She recovers nicely. *Kanhorre!*"

KNAI"DLACH, Dumplings made of Matza meal served (usually) with soup at the Saider Service. Used as a proverb: "He does not mean the *Haggadah*, he means the *Knaidlach*." — All he wants is to get some material gain. (The *Haggadah* is the ritual part of the *Saider* preceding the meal.)

KUNTZ, A clever act, a trick, a gimmick.

KU"GEL, Pudding, made from potatoes, or from noodles, especially prepared for the Sabbath meal.

MER"TSHE-SHEM (corruption of Hebrew *Im-Yirtze-haShem*), "If God wills so." Frequently heard in Jewish Parlance. Ex.: "I'll come, *Mertshe Shem*."

MIL"CHEG (see *Fleishig*), Food produced from milk or containing a dairy ingredient.

NAHR, A fool. NAHRISH, Foolish, stupid.

NEB"BICH, Of doubtful origin it implies pity and compassion.

NISHT-KO"SHE (combination of German-Hebrew), Not so hard, not bad, passable.

NUD"NIK, A bore, a nuisance, a pest.

OI GEVALT"!, Exclamation of suffering or surprise. "Oh, dear!"

PASKUDNIK (Slavic), A disgraceful, nasty person.

PAR"VE, Food which is neither *Milchig* nor *Fleishig*, and may be eaten with meat or milk.

PUSH"KE, Charity box. Jewish homes have had one or more such boxes placed there by various charity or national organizations, such as the Jewish National Fund, or for the upkeep of some charitable institution. On some occasions, especially before kindling the Sabbath lights, coins are dropped inside (to be later collected by representatives of the various organizations).

REB"BE, See Rabbi.
REB"BETZIN, Rabbi's wife.
SHAI"TEL, A wig worn by pious women.
SHLACH-MOO"NES (corruption from Hebrew *Mishloach Manoth*), Gifts sent on *Purim*, usually accompanied by pastry and confections.
SHLEMI"EL or SHLIM-MAZEL (*Shlim*—in German; bad. *Mazal*—in Hebrew; luck. Thus one of ill-luck, or hard luck), a simpleton.
SHLE"PPER, Beggar, sponger, parasite.
SHMA"TTE, A rag, worthless.
SHNAPS, A drink of whisky.
SHNOR"RER, A beggar.
TZIM"MES, Desert, also used: to make a fuss over nothing.
TSHU"LENT, Sabbath noon dish. As no cooking is allowed on the Sabbath, food consisting of meat, potatoes, or *Kasha*, or beans are put into a hot oven and allowed to bake until the Sabbath noon meal. A special part of the *Tshulent* is the *Kugel*.
TZU GEZUNT", or GESUNDHAIT!, To health! (Usually exclaimed at someone who is sneezing.)
YAHR"ZEIT, Anniversary of the death of a person. On that date, the nearest of kin recite *Kaddish* during the daily prayer. (Also some other customs are observed.)

THE THIRTEEN PRINCIPLES OF THE JEWISH FAITH*

1. I believe with perfect faith that the Creator, blessed be his name, is the Author and Guide of everything that has been created, and that he alone has made, does make, and will make all things.

2. I believe with perfect faith that the Creator, blessed be his name, is a Unity, and that there is no unity in any manner like unto his, and that he alone is our God, who was, is, and will be.

3. I believe with perfect faith that the Creator, blessed be his name, is not a body, and that he is free from all the accidents of matter, and that he has not any form whatsoever.

4. I believe with perfect faith that the Creator, blessed be his name, is the first and the last.

5. I believe with perfect faith that to the Creator, blessed be his name, and to him alone, it is right to pray, and that it is not right to pray to any being besides him.

*These Articles of the Jewish Creed were formulated by Moses Maimonides in the 12th Century C.E. They are recited at the end of the daily morning service.

6. I believe with perfect faith that all the words of the pro-
    phets are true.

7. I believe with perfect faith that the prophecy of Moses,
    our teacher, peace be unto him, was true, and that he was
    the chief of the prophets, both of those that preceded and
    of those that followed him.

8. I believe with perfect faith that the whole Law, now in
    our possession, is the same that was given to Moses our
    teacher, peace be unto him.

9. I believe with perfect faith that this Law will not be
    changed, and that there will never be any other law from
    the Creator, blessed be his name.

10. I believe with perfect faith that the Creator, blessed be his
    name, knows every deed of the children of men, and all
    their thoughts, as it is said, It is he that fashioneth the
    hearts of them all, that giveth heed to all their deeds.

11. I believe with perfect faith that the Creator, blessed be his
    name, rewards those that keep his commandments, and
    punishes those that transgress them.

12. I believe with perfect faith in the coming of the Messiah,
    and, though he tarry, I will wait daily for his coming.

13. I believe with perfect faith that there will be a resurrection
    of the dead at the time when it shall please the Creator,
    blessed be his name, and exalted be the remembrance of
    him for ever and ever.